MALCOLM X

MAKE

IT

PLAIN

MALCOLM X

MAKE

IT

PLAIN

Text by
WILLIAM STRICKLAND

Oral histories selected and edited by
CHERYLL Y. GREENE

with the Malcolm X Documentary Production Team
Picture Research by Michele McKenzie

PENGUIN BOOKS

PENGUIN BOOKS
Published by the Penguin Group
Penguin Books USA Inc., 375 Hudson Street, New York, New York 10014, U.S.A.
Penguin Books Ltd, 27 Wrights Lane, London W8 5TZ, England
Penguin Books Australia Ltd, Ringwood, Victoria, Australia
Penguin Books Canada Ltd, 10 Alcorn Avenue, Toronto, Ontario, Canada M4V 3B2
Penguin Books (N.Z.) Ltd, 182–190 Wairau Road, Auckland 10, New Zealand

Penguin Books Ltd, Registered Offices: Harmondsworth, Middlesex, England

First published in the United States of America by Viking Penguin,
a division of Penguin Books USA Inc., 1994
Published in Penguin Books 1995

1 3 5 7 9 10 8 6 4 2

Grateful acknowledgment is made for permission to reprint excerpts from
The Autobiography of Malcolm X by Malcolm X, with the assistance of Alex Haley.
Copyright © 1964 by Alex Haley and Malcolm X. Copyright © 1965 by Alex Haley
and Betty Shabazz. Reprinted by permission of Random House, Inc.

Photograph credits appear on pages 241–244.

THE LIBRARY OF CONGRESS HAS CATALOGUED THE HARDCOVER AS FOLLOWS:
Strickland, William.
Malcolm X: Make It Plain/text by William Strickland; with the Malcolm X:
Make It Plain production team, and Cheryll Y. Greene.
p.   cm.
Includes bibliographical references.
ISBN 0-670-84893-X (hc.)
ISBN 0 14 017.713 2 (pbk.)
1. X, Malcolm, 1925–1965—Pictorial works. 2. X, Malcolm, 1925–1965.
3. Black Muslims—Biography. 4. Afro-Americans—Biography. I. Title.
BP223.Z8L5776 1994
320.5´4´092—dc20   [B]   93–6297

Printed in the United States of America
Set in Gill Sans and Cochin
Designed by Brian Mulligan and Guenet Abraham

"'Make it plain' is the code that he used for us
to bring him forward. He didn't like
a lot of icing, you know."

—Benjamin Karim, describing how he introduced
Malcolm X at public gatherings

ACKNOWLEDGMENTS

Presenting the story of Malcolm X has been a difficult but remarkably rewarding undertaking. This book is based on the interviews and research conducted for the documentary program that Blackside produced in conjunction with the PBS series *The American Experience*.

This book is the work of a dedicated team of publishing professionals. Cheryll Y. Greene took the project on and made it a labor of love. She worked with great intensity and energy in New York, meeting with us in Boston when she could, relying on express delivery, faxes, and the telephone when she could not. She worked through the difficult challenges posed by bringing together the many elements of this book. She acted as a consulting editor throughout the process of developing the essays for this book, and her skills and vision were crucial to their realization. She also showed her talents in her selection and captioning of the two hundred photographs included here.

William Strickland embraced the challenge of writing of Malcolm's life and he did so in spite of the numerous scheduling constraints placed upon a project whose release must coincide with a broadcast date. We owe him a debt of thanks for his patience, persistence, and willingness to cooperate. Bill's perspectives helped us all, on the film and book teams, to understand better what it was we were trying to accomplish.

Michele McKenzie traveled by train, plane, car, and cab relentlessly in search of photographs that offer fresh insight into the story of Malcolm X's life. She showed remarkable skill at collecting photographs that have never or rarely been seen.

The team members on this book worked under the direction of Robert Lavelle. He has led and directed the creation and production of all of Blackside's publications for eight years and his work has been extraordinary. With patience and sensitivity, he has handled delicate matters with a powerful intelligence and a rich sense of humor. This work would not have happened without him.

We sorely taxed the good graces, patience, and wisdom of our editor at Viking, Dawn Seferian. Fortunately she possesses these qualities in abundance. To Beena Kamlani, Amy Hill, Brian Mulligan and the other talented professionals in Viking's production department, we offer our thanks for their flexibility, persistence, and thorough professionalism.

Our literary agent, Doe Coover, worked with us closely on developing the book project and then on helping us make the publishing process successful.

Judy Richardson, co-producer of the documentary film, reviewed the manuscript and made numerous suggestions and contributions. Her sensitivity to the political and cultural nuances of Malcolm's life and her boundless energy and enthusiasm for her subject are unmatched.

Gerald Gill of Tufts University was one of the most helpful of those who commented on early versions of this project. He offered many helpful suggestions. We're grateful as well to John A. Williams for his participation in the first stages of this book project. Judy Crichton and Margaret Drain, of *The American Experience*, informed our book project through their valuable insights into the documentary film. To all who offered their critical perspectives we offer thanks.

Others on the book team who helped were: Neeti Madan and Marpessa Dawn Outlaw (assistant editors); Leila Fergus, Aleta Alston, and Suzanne Leake (editorial assistants); Denise Greene and Meredith Woods (film production staff who helped with general research and Meredith, with book research); Bridgette Dunn, Susan Cho, Nikki Richards, Ginger Beverly, and Barnard Jaffier (interns).

We would particularly like to thank the underwriters for the film project: *The American Experience*, The Ford Foundation, Corporation for Public Broadcasting, and Camille O. Cosby and William H. Cosby, Jr. Without their support our work could not go forward.

This book project began because Ruth Batson of the Ruth M. Batson Educational Foundation gave us a grant enabling us to think through our project, develop it, and find a publisher. To that foundation's board of trustees we offer a special thanks. We are contributing a portion of any eventual earnings from this project to a scholarship fund for African American youth. The fund will be administered by the Ruth M. Batson Educational Foundation.

Lastly, we want to express our gratitude to the people who shared with us their memories of the life and times of Malcolm X. Your willingness to pass on your history to others and to future generations adds to the legacy of the life of one of this century's most remarkable leaders.

—Henry Hampton, Executive Producer; President, Blackside, Inc.
Orlando Bagwell, Producer, Director and Co-Writer
of the documentary film *Malcolm X: Make It Plain*.

CONTENTS

MESSENGER MALCOLM

"I fought the best that I knew how . . ."

Malcolm X, 1964

In the beginning, the Bible tells us, was the Word. But for me, and for the generation that came to consciousness in the sixties, the Word that created our new beginning (and America's) was "Black." And the not-to-be trifled-with Giver of the Word was Malcolm X.

Before Malcolm, the relationship between Black people and America was equivocal, elliptical, elusive—and dishonest. It was the Age of the Negro, an era of pseudoracial "peace," upon which Malcolm exploded like a wanton shellburst and changed forever the way that "Negroes" and America thought about themselves and one another.

Before Malcolm, most of us, Black and white alike, basked in the aura of American goodness. It was something we took for granted and never, therefore, basically questioned. We tended to think of the country as we thought of ourselves: as immortal, as special, as flowing on . . . like a river. In fact, despite our periodic misgivings, frustrations, and exasperations with her sins and foibles, Black folk tended to identify with America most of all. Back then, whoever might call us "Black" or "African" would probably, almost surely, have a fight on his or her hands.

In those days, few of us had thought very deeply about race, because beginning in the mid-fifties, race seemed an about-to-be-conquered problem in America. The Supreme Court had ruled favorably in the *Brown* decision, restrictive covenants were being struck down almost routinely, the NAACP had embarked on its ten-year plan—Free by '63—to coincide with the centennial of the Emancipation Proclamation, while in the South, the Montgomery bus boycott had triumphed and a new young Black leader, Dr. Martin Luther King, Jr., had emerged.

Then . . . along came Malcolm, burning down our straw-filled beliefs with his mocking fire words.

He stung our consciences and awakened our minds. Taken aback, we would stammer, bluster, lash back, talk about his mama. But deep down, we knew that his questions were real and that we did not have real answers for them. He was—and there is no other honest way to put this—our spiritual and intellectual father, breathing into us a new mental and racial life. And pride was only part of it.

Where we were stumbling, Malcolm picked us up. Where we were confused, Malcolm illuminated. Where we were timid, Malcolm emboldened. Malcolm was the Messenger's Messenger, but he was *our* prophet, *our* crusader, *our* heretic, *our* big brother. If they insulted us, he sprang to our defense. If they lied, he exposed. If they slandered, he ridiculed. And if they injured, he threatened. Ossie Davis has called Malcolm "our Black shining prince," but he was also our champion, the Joe Louis / Muhammad Ali of our time, knocking out chump challengers who dared to enter the intellectual ring against him with the blows that rendered them defenseless: the truths of Western and American history.

From the very beginning of America's history, racism has been its deepest shadow. More than any other force, race has divided the American people, subverted the country's fullest potential, and mothballed our dreams. The wrongs committed in its name over four hundred years have been incalculable, destroying or damaging countless lives. But from the very beginning, America failed to acknowledge this deepest flaw. . . . Until Malcolm.

It was Malcolm who redefined the discourse on race in this country. He moved the discussion from notions of "prejudice" and "discrimination" and "civil rights" to racism. It was Malcolm who broadcast concepts like "community control" and "white power structure" (taking the blame out of the realm of the amorphous and popularizing a whole new vocabulary with which to help Blacks interpret and combat their condition). It was Malcolm who insisted that the problem was not civil rights but human rights. And it was Malcolm who made it clear that Blacks were victims of a *system* of domination and exploitation that was not regional but national, not superficial but structural, not episodic but ongoing and intentional. "Stop talking about the South," he would say. "When you cross the Canadian border you're in the 'South.'"

Malcolm pulled the covers off the concealed dynamic of race and political reality in America. His unflinching critical comparison of what was with what was supposed to be is what gave Malcolm his moral authority. He would "tell it like it is." And then ask: "Is that right or wrong?"

How he gained such clarity and then passed it on to others is the true significance of Malcolm X, a significance that defines the essence of leadership in his time and ours.

THE
HISTORY
THAT MADE
MALCOLM

"Make way for Democracy! We saved it in France, and by the Great Jehovah, we will save it in the U.S.A., or know the reason why."

W. E. B. Du Bois, *The Crisis*, May 1919

Because of the tremendous power of Malcolm's personality and his undeniable impact upon American thought and identity, we tend to think of him as being someone above history rather than someone who shaped and was shaped by it. Yet the Malcolm X we know is unimaginable apart from the family into which he was born and the

Facing page: 1963

parents who gave him life. He is unimaginable apart from the Garveyism to which his parents were committed and the Garveyism out of which the Nation of Islam sprang; and he is unimaginable apart from the American racism that radicalized him as it radicalized so many who have wrestled with being both Black and human in a persistently resistant America.

GARVEYISM: THE NATION BEFORE THE "NATION" (1920–25)

In August 1920, Madison Square Garden hosted an event unlike any that had been seen in America before or since; twenty-five thousand multihued Black persons, representing twenty-five countries and four continents, gathered in New York to attend the First International Convention of the Negro Peoples of the World. Organized by Jamaican-born Marcus Garvey under the auspices of his Universal Negro Improvement Association (UNIA), the Great Convention elected Garvey Provisional President of Africa, adopted a Declaration of the Rights of the Negro Peoples of the World, and marked Garvey as leader of the largest mass organization in the history of the African Diaspora.

This Pan-African assembly deliberated in New York throughout the month of August. In its name and in the name of the "four hundred million Negroes of the world," Garvey sent a telegram of support to Eamon de Valera, president of the Irish Republic, endorsing the Irish struggle for independence from Great Britain. The telegram declared, in cadences that foreshadowed the Black Panther party of the 1960s: "Ireland for the Irish, Europe for the Europeans, and Africa for the Black people of the world."

Then, having addressed white political matters, the Black Parliament turned its attention to the question of worldwide racial discrimination, approving Article 20 of the Declaration of Rights, which stated: "We protest against segregated districts, separate public

...day, February 22, 2005

Malcolm X remembered at theater where he was killed

Associated Press

NEW YORK—The Manhattan theater where Malcolm X was assassinated held a commemoration on Monday, the 40th anniversary of the civil rights leader's death.

The Audubon Ballroom, where the activist was gunned down Feb. 21, 1965, is being turned into a history center named for him and his wife that will re-examine his life and legacy by cataloging his life and work and showing how he was a champion of human rights, his family said.

Dignitaries who attended the event Monday evening included Mayor Michael Bloomberg, Rep. Charles Rangel and the Rev. Al Sharpton.

"Malcolm didn't build buildings or pass legislation," Sharpton said. "He taught us how to think. And when he changed our minds, we could build buildings and we could pass legislation."

The official opening of the Malcolm X and Dr. Betty Shabazz Memorial and Education Center is slated for May 19, his 80th birthday.

The center will house a multimedia environment containing documents about Malcolm X's life, including memoirs, notes and speeches rescued by his family and held by the Schomburg Center for Research in Black Culture in Harlem.

The collection will "enlighten a lot of people," said Malaak Shabazz, whose mother was pregnant with her and her twin sister, Malikah Shabazz, when their father was slain.

...ion, lynching and limitations of ...en in any part of the world on ...will exert our full influence and ...ntiments thus expressed so ...tedly, he suggested a postscript ...ve democracy in this country if

...dered a declaration of rights, a ...u of Investigation just the year ...radical, potentially subversive, ...as John Edgar Hoover, and he ...tions by immediately instituting ...racial-advancement or Black ...quality" or "equal rights." He ...ding an "appropriate crime"

...charging Garvey with being ...ey toyed with the idea of ...sporting a woman across a ...been used so successfully ...weight champion Jack Johnson. Finally, after nearly three years of cogitating, they indicted Garvey in 1922 on charges of mail fraud.

Convicted in 1923, Garvey was sent to the Atlanta Federal Penitentiary in 1925—the year that one of his most devoted followers, Mrs. Louise Little, gave birth, in Omaha, Nebraska, to her fourth child by Reverend Earl Little. The infant was named Malcolm. So, serendipitously, Hoover had gotten rid of the most dangerous radical of one era, only to have his successor appear, as if by divine racial command.

MALCOLM'S FIRST FAMILY (1925–40)

We do not know much about Malcolm's parents, except that his mother, Louise Norton Little, immigrated to Montreal, Canada, from the British West Indian colony of Grenada, where she was the unacknowledged offspring of a white Scot and a Grenadian woman. She was said to have been attractive and fair-skinned.

Earl Little had been born in Georgia in 1890. He grew to manhood in the Peach State, entered into a youthful marriage that produced three children, and then left Georgia and his first family, to migrate to Canada. (Because of the work made available by the Canadian Pacific Railroad, Montreal was a miniature version of Garvey's Pan-African world. Garvey even came to Montreal in 1919 to inform his supporters of the forthcoming International Convention in New York. Did Earl and Louise hear him? Were they members of the Montreal UNIA then? We know only that they met in Montreal and married in May 1919, exactly six years before Malcolm was born.)

As in the case of Malcolm's mother, we have scant information about Earl Little. But we do know what the Jim Crow South was like in the years before Little left it, because we have the expert testimony of white and Black witnesses, like Edgar Gardner Murphy and W. E. B. Du Bois.

As America slipped into the twentieth century, Murphy wrote that "southern extremists proceeded from an undiscriminating attack upon the Negro's ballot to a like attack upon his schools, his labor, his life— from the contention that no Negro shall labor, that no Negro shall learn, and (by implication) that no Negro shall live."

What Murphy's observation meant in concrete terms we can gather from Du Bois's hastening home to protect his family from the Atlanta Pogrom of 1906, when Georgia citizens, celebrating the success of their September disenfranchising convention, indulged in an orgy of bloodletting that lasted three days and killed eleven Blacks. So we think we understand why Earl Little left Georgia . . . and America.

What is more difficult to understand is why Little would leave Canada with a young bride who could be mistaken for white, to return to an America still blood-soaked from the "Red Summer" of 1919, a summer in which seventy-eight Blacks, including ten World War I soldiers, had been lynched.

This terrorism was intended to convey the message to the new Black urban dwellers and returning veterans that nothing had changed in the world for which the veterans had fought to make it "safe for democracy."

But perhaps Earl Little returned precisely because of this racial turmoil; maybe he took heart from the fact that racial clashes in America were no longer so one-sided and Blacks were fighting back! In twenty-five locales across the country—in Longview, Texas, and in Chester, Pennsylvania; in Omaha, Nebraska, and Knoxville, Tennessee; in Elaine, Arkansas, and in the nation's capital of Washington, D.C.—Blacks were fighting back. Indeed, in Chicago the races slugged it out for nearly two weeks, with Blacks giving as good as they got—fighting back! These, the first urban rebellions of this century, only confirmed the attitude of the "New Negroes" who appeared, battle-ready, in the urban centers of postwar America long before they became identified primarily with the literary Harlem Renaissance.

It is also possible that Little came back to participate in the First International Convention of the Negro Peoples of the World, since we know that the couple's first child, Wilfred, was born in Philadelphia a few months before the convention was launched, and Philadelphia was but a hop, skip, and jump from the convention site in New York.

Were the Littles among the convention's number? If they were, it would confirm something Malcolm later said about his father: that he wasn't "a frightened Negro." We might then wonder whether this refusal to be intimidated was somehow passed along from father to son—a predisposition to enter the fray in behalf of one's people against all odds and "by any means necessary."

Accepting the thrown gauntlet seems, in fact, to have been the infectious spirit of the time. It was the sentiment behind the editorial, quoted above, that Du Bois published in *The Crisis* in the very month the Littles married in Montreal. Was that the call they heard, the call to which they responded?

> We return from the slavery of uniform which the world's madness demanded us to don to the freedom of civil garb. We stand again to look America squarely in the face and call a spade a spade. We sing: This country of ours, despite all its better souls have done and dreamed, is yet a shameful land.
>
> It lynches. . . . It disenfranchises its own citizens. . . . It encourages ignorance. . . . It steals from us. . . . It insults us. . . .
>
> We RETURN. We return FROM FIGHTING. We RETURN FIGHTING.
>
> Make way for Democracy! We saved it in France, and by the Great Jehovah, we will save it in the U.S.A., or know the reason why.

ON THE ROAD

In the first six years of Malcolm's life, the Little family, hard-pressed by a declining economy, which would soon implode into a full-blown national depression, and pressured by Klan hostility to Earl and Louise Little's UNIA politics, moved at least four times: from Omaha, Nebraska, to Milwaukee, Wisconsin, to Lansing and finally to East Lansing, Michigan. The family seemed always on the move (a pattern Malcolm would repeat nearly all his adult life—save for those years when he was an involuntary ward of the prison system of the State of Massachusetts).

The move from Omaha, Malcolm's birthplace, was occasioned, Malcolm recounts in his *Autobiography,* by an incident that occurred before he was born.

One night while his father was away preaching, his mother later told him, Klansmen appeared at their door and warned Malcolm's mother that "the 'good, Christian white people' were not going to stand for my father's 'spreading trouble' among the 'good Negroes' of Omaha with the 'Back to Africa' teachings of Marcus Garvey."

Earl Little was then president of the Omaha branch of the UNIA, and Louise Little was responsible for sending news of chapter activities to Garvey's international newspaper, *The Negro World*. The Littles seem to have been successful enough in their political work to have organized a Liberty Hall meeting place in Omaha, and this, presumably, had aroused the Klan's ire. After Malcolm was born, therefore, the family left Omaha for Milwaukee.

To appreciate why the Littles moved, one must appreciate the enormous political influence of the Ku Klux Klan during this period. Reorganized at the outbreak of World War I, the Klan elected governors, congressmen, and senators. It had millions of members and cultivated "law enforcement" contacts everywhere it could—not only in the South but in New England, Oregon, Indiana, Michigan, and other northern, western, and midwestern states. (In fact, in 1925, three months after Malcolm's birth, the Klan marched down Pennsylvania Avenue forty-thousand strong and twenty-five abreast for four hours, as a show of strength. And the year before, they had almost elected a presidential nominee in Madison Square Garden, where Garvey had convened the Great Convention of 1920. Meeting in the same month of August, the Klan forced the Democratic party into the longest convention in its history, sixteen days—and 103 ballots!—before the Klan-supported candidate gave way to the compromise choice, John W. Davis—who would later argue against Thurgood Marshall in the 1954 school desegregation case we all now know as *Brown* v. *Board of Education of Topeka*.)

So the Littles moved, but they didn't abandon their politics. In Milwaukee, for example, Earl Little was president of the International Industrial Club of Milwaukee, which in 1927 sent a letter to President Calvin Coolidge requesting a pardon for Marcus Garvey. In 1929, Little bought a house in Lansing in a white neighborhood and was promptly served with an eviction notice because a restrictive covenant in his purchase agreement prohibited "anyone other than persons of the Caucasian race" from renting or buying the house. Two months after the Littles were taken to court, the house, according to Malcolm, was burned to the ground by whites who resented his father's violation of the housing taboos, as well as his desire to open a store in the town.

Thus we have a picture of Earl Little as a man trying to practice what he preached. He was trying "to do for self" by starting his own business; and he also claimed his right as a citizen to live anywhere he could afford. Then, when his home was torched, he moved his family to a six-acre site in East Lansing ("we want some land of our own") and built them a four-room home himself. Louise Little worked to instill personal and race pride in her children: She read with them from *The Negro World* and the daily newspaper; she told them stories about their ancestry; and she insisted that they refer to themselves not as *Negroes* but as *Black people.* In both Earl and Louise Little, then, we see traits that will reappear in Malcolm's character: a spirit of independence, a refusal to be intimidated, an innate Black pride, and a resourcefulness. Obviously, such a Black man as Earl Little, who would not "stay in his place" and who spread the racial gospel even after Garvey had been deported and after he himself had been warned, was risking his life. Not surprisingly, then, in September 1931, Earl Little was mysteriously run over by an East Lansing trolley car. The police called it an accident. Malcolm believed it was murder.

This calamity left Louise Little a widow with seven children in the tag end of a Depression year when Black unemployment was 35 percent. With the help of the oldest children, Wilfred and Hilda, she struggled to keep the family together, working as a seamstress and doing housework. But the strain wore her down. Inexorably, the humiliation of being forced to seek public assistance, and the ever mounting challenge of making ends meet when you have no ends to start with, eroded her spirit.

The children struggled on as best they could, but by the seventh grade Malcolm began to have trouble and was expelled. He became something of a troublemaker and wound up in a white juvenile home in Mason, Michigan. Unexpectedly, Malcolm adjusted well in Mason, both to his white caretakers and to his school, where he was very popular. He later credited some of this popularity to the fact that he was the "token" Black in the school, but he had begun to demonstrate his native intelligence and natural leadership ability. He was ranked third in his class and elected class president. He did have a run-in with one of his teachers who sang "coon songs," but this warning shot fired across his racial bow faded into the background when his half sister Ella Collins, who had "made it" in Boston, arrived for a visit.

Ella was a revelation to Malcolm. He said that she was the first really *Black* person he had met who was proud of her dark complexion. (Did she remind him of the motto he had heard at the meetings his father sometimes took him to: "Up, you mighty race, you can accomplish what you will"?) At any rate, when Ella extended an invitation to visit her in Boston, Malcolm said he "jumped at it."

When Malcolm first came to Boston, in the summer of 1940, he was fifteen years old, a self-described "country hick from Mason, Michigan." The Black Roxbury neighborhood was, therefore, a revelation he found so exhilarating and intoxicating that "I couldn't have feigned indifference if I had tried to. People talked casually about Chicago, Detroit, New York. I didn't know the world contained as many Negroes as I saw thronging downtown Roxbury at night, especially on Saturdays. Neon lights, nightclubs, pool halls, bars, the cars they drove!"

Malcolm was hooked. When he returned to Mason, he wrote Ella "almost every day." He was "restless" with Mason and "with being around white people." Roxbury, the racial Mecca, had fired his blood beyond cooling. He had to return—like his father before him—to the flame. (He did not, of course, know that far away across the Atlantic, the man who had inspired his father and mother and who had made "Race!" a beacon that had thrilled so many—as it was now thrilling Malcolm—had died in London of a cerebral hemorrhage. Marcus Garvey was dead at fifty-three.)

In Their Own Words

Florentine Baril	Widow of Officer Lawrence Baril, the state trooper who was called to the scene where Earl Little, Malcolm's father, died
Ella Collins	Malcolm's elder half sister
Belva Cotton	Junior high school classmate in Mason, Michigan
Jim Cotton	Junior high school classmate in Mason, Michigan
Wilfred Little	Malcolm's eldest brother
Cyril McGuire	Childhood friend in Lansing
Abdul Aziz Omar	Formerly Philbert Little, Malcolm's second elder brother
Jenny Washington	Childhood friend in Lansing
Yvonne Little Woodward	Malcolm's younger sister

My mother was the teacher. She didn't tolerate us being treated as a negative or as subhuman. She told us we came from great people that were onetime rulers.

Abdul Aziz Omar

Well, my father was dark-complected, about six foot four in height, no fat—muscle and bone, as they used to call him—a very strong man, not only physically, in other ways too. He had come out of Georgia, where he'd grown up on a farm.

Wilfred Little

Malcolm's parents, Earl and Louise Little.

A detail from Malcolm's fourth-grade class picture, Lansing, 1935–36.

At night before we would go to bed, we would all gather around the stove, and my mother would tell us stories. Or we would sing our alphabets, or we would sing our math, and then she taught us French—we could sing in French. And then she would tell us stories about our ancestry.

Abdul Aziz Omar

Klanvocation at Lansing, Michigan, 1924, the year before Malcolm was born.

Harlem parade, ca. 1925. "The New Negro" spirit of the Garvey
movement and the Harlem Renaissance meet at 135th Street and
Lenox Avenue around the time of Malcolm's birth.

Life in Lansing,
Michigan, 1920s.
Top: Rural scene.
Middle: Masonic
Lodge, Red Union
Club show.
Bottom: Looking
toward the Capitol
building.

Malcolm (*top row, fifth from right*) in Lansing elementary school class picture, probably 1934–35.

People saw us as oddballs in the city where we grew up. Whites would refer to us as "those uppity niggers" or "those smart niggers" that live out south of town. In those days whenever a white person referred to you as a smart nigger, that was their way of saying this is someone you had to watch, he catches on to things. . . .

In those days, the twenties and thirties, it was the same as being in Mississippi. A lot of people don't know this. When you went into the courts and when you had to deal with the police, it was the same as being down south.

Wilfred Little

When we went to school, we were the only Blacks in the school. This had its problems, but we were continuously buoyed up by our parents, so we were able to deal with it. Even in those days you opened school with the national anthem and the Pledge of Allegiance first thing in the morning. One morning I told the teacher—I said we got a national anthem too, Black has got a national anthem. She says, "Well, get up there and sing it." So I got up and sang it, but what it really was was an anthem we would sing whenever we had meetings in the UNIA, which was Universal Negro Improvement Association that Marcus Garvey had established. It began with words like, uh, "Ethiopia, the land of the free, the land where the gods used to be . . ." and on from there. That created some problems, because here is this little nigger that feels he is just equal to anybody else, he got his own little national anthem that he sings, and he's proud of it, and the words to it fit what he thinks. It wasn't the way they wanted things to go.

Wilfred Little

A Garveyite family,
Harlem, 1920s.

We were burned out in Lansing, Michigan, because they sold my father a home they were not supposed to sell to Blacks. We're talking about the state capital. The house burned down to the ground—no fire wagon came, nothing. At the time, my father took a shot at somebody who he said was running away from the house, and they arrested him and put him in jail because he shot at that person. I understood that somebody had thrown gasoline or something all over the kitchen and lit it and it blew up, and it woke my mother up. She got us outta the house, otherwise we would've all been cremated.

Abdul Aziz Omar

All of a sudden we heard a big boom. When we woke up, fire was everywhere, and everybody was running into the walls and into each other, trying to get away. I could hear my mother yelling, my father yelling—they made sure they got us all rounded up and got us out. The fire was spreadin' so fast that they couldn't hardly bring anything else out. My mother began to run back and bring out bedclothing, whatever she could grab, and pulled it to the porch and then out into the yard. She made the mistake of laying my baby sister down on top of some quilts and things that were there and then went back for something else. When she came back, she didn't see the baby—what had happened, they'd put somethin' else on top of the baby. And my mother almost lost her mind. I mean they were hanging on to her to keep her from going back into the house. And then finally the baby cried, and they knew where the baby was.

Wilfred Little

In those days if you were looked upon in the community as a Negro who wouldn't back down, who did your own thinking and just didn't submit to whatever they wanted to put on you, they would what they call blackball you. They'd go to wherever you were employed and ask them to fire you. So knowing that my father didn't intend to stop what he was doing—he was always speaking in terms of Marcus Garvey's way of thinking and trying to get Black people to organize themselves to work in unity toward improving their conditions—in those days if you did that, you were still considered a troublemaker.

Wilfred Little

My father didn't want anybody to exercise authority over his children. He wanted to exercise the authority, and he did. And he didn't want anyone to sell him some house that was worn out. He wanted his own home, and he built it.

Abdul Aziz Omar

On our land we produced everything that we needed—everything we needed to eat, we produced it right there. Plus some to sell on the market, and my mother would can some to carry us through the winters. This kept us more or less in an independent mode.

Wilfred Little

Marcus Garvey (*center*) in plumed hat, and officers review a UNIA parade, Harlem, 1920s.

Back in those days in the city of Lansing there was no such thing as a UNIA hall. So my father would get together people who were interested, and they would go in cars to Detroit, and in Detroit we'd have a chance to attend meetings where they would have speakers. Sometimes he would take me, or he would take Malcolm—the ones that were old enough to kinda understand.

When you'd leave there you'd feel proud of yourself, you know—you'd be proud that you were Black. You knew that you had been somebody and you're gon' be somebody now if you got the chance, and you looked for every opportunity to accomplish that.

Wilfred Little

MICHIGAN DEPARTMENT OF HEALTH
Division of Vital Statistics
CERTIFICATE OF DEATH

State Office No. 133 8243

1 PLACE OF DEATH
County Ingham
Township Lansing
Village
City Lansing
(No. Sparrow Hospital
(If death occurred in a hospital or institution, give its NAME instead of street and number)
Register No. 545
Ward)

2 FULL NAME Earl Little
(a) Residence No. Lansing Township St., Ward
(Usual place of abode) (If non-resident give city or town and state)
Length of residence in city or town where death occurred 20 yrs. mos. ds. How long in U. S., if of foreign birth? yrs. mos. ds.

PERSONAL AND STATISTICAL PARTICULARS

3 SEX Male
4 Color or Race Colored
5 Single, Married, Widowed or Divorced (WRITE the word) Married
5a If married, widowed or divorced HUSBAND of (or) WIFE of Louise Little
6 DATE OF BIRTH (Month, day and year) July 29, 1890
7 AGE Years 41 Months 2 Days 0 If LESS than 1 day ___ hrs. OR ___ min.

OCCUPATION
8. Trade, profession, or particular kind of work done, as spinner, sawyer, bookkeeper, etc. Minister
9. Industry or business in which work was done, as silk mill, saw mill, bank, etc.
10. Date deceased last work at this occupation (month and year) Sept. 28, 1931
11. Total time (years) spent in this occupation 25

12. BIRTHPLACE (city or town) Butler
(State or country) Georgia

FATHER
13. NAME John Little
14. BIRTHPLACE (city or town) Unknown
(State or country) Georgia

MOTHER
15. MAIDEN NAME Unknown
16. BIRTHPLACE (city or town) Unknown
(State or country) Georgia

17. INFORMANT Louise Little
(Address) Lansing Township

18. BURIAL, CREMATION, OR REMOVAL
Place Reynolds Cemetery Date Oct. 2, 1931

19. UNDERTAKER
(Address)

20. FILED 9-30, 1931 Registrar.

MEDICAL CERTIFICATE OF DEATH

21. DATE OF DEATH (month, day, and year) Sept 28 1931
22. I HEREBY CERTIFY, That I attended deceased from ___, 19___, to ___, 19___
I last saw h___ alive on ___, 19___; death is said to have occurred on the date stated above, at 4:50 p.m.
The principal cause of death and related causes of importance were as follows:
Internal injuries left arm and left leg fury crushed when run over by a M. E. R. Street car

DURATION

Other contributory causes of importance:

If operation, date of
Condition for which performed
Organ or part affected
Was there laboratory test? Autopsy? No.
In case of violence state if accident, homicide or suicide
Accident
Where did injury occur? E. Mich Ave & Detroit St
Lansing Township (Specify city, county or state) Ingham Co.
In industry, home or public place?
Was disease or injury related to occupation of deceased? No.
Signed W. Ray Loveland Coroner M.D.
Address Lansing

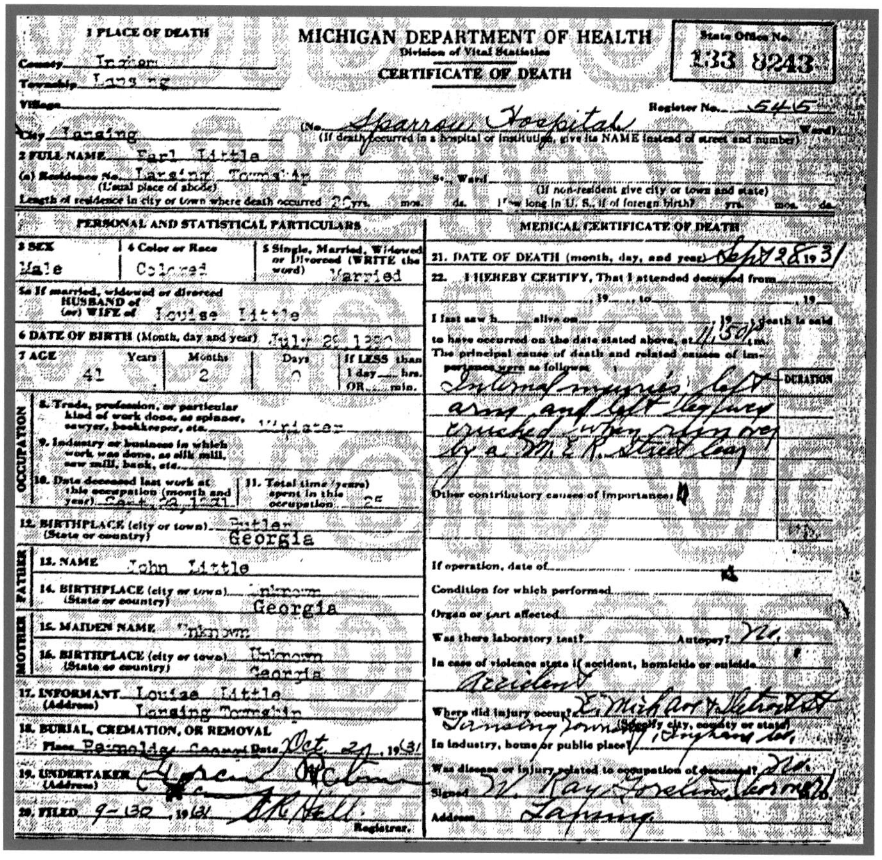

Earl Little's death certificate.

My father's death caused a great, great shock in the family, because he was the power—he was the strength. We were organized. We were a structured family. When we got out of school, me and my brothers and sisters, we'd come right home and go to work in the garden, clean up the chicken shed, and get ready for the night. We'd pump the water and bring it in the house and all this. To not do this brought the consequence of a whipping. Everybody knew what they had to do and did it. We children were under check.

Abdul Aziz Omar

When it was known that he was dead, white people, Black people, everybody came to the funeral. All of a sudden he becomes a big hero. In those days we used to have a saying among Black people about how white people would just come and praise the person when he's dead—they had a saying, "A dead nigger is a good nigger." All of a sudden they don't mind giving him credit for being a brave and an honorable man, a man who stood up for what he believed in.

Wilfred Little

When it comes to my father's death, there's a lot of mystery around it. My father was killed by a streetcar. We were all at the house, and we had supper together, and my mother was holding Wesley, who's my youngest brother, and she may have been nursing him, 'cause she was at the table and she fell asleep, nursing, holding the baby. And my father had gotten up and went in the bedroom to clean up and to go to the north side of Lansing and collect chicken money.

She woke up and said, "Earl, Earl, don't go downtown. If you go, you won't come back." And so my father said, "Oh, Louise, get away." And she said, "Earl, please don't go." But he left. We all finally went to bed, and late that night somebody banged on the door—and my mother screamed, she said, "Earl!" like that. And the police said, "Louise Little, your husband has been injured. Would you come with us please." They claimed my father lived two and a half hours after he had been run over. But when she got there, he was dead.

I heard that somebody had hit my father from behind with a car and knocked him under the streetcar. Then I learned later that somebody had shoved him under that car. What actually happened, I don't know.

Abdul Aziz Omar

Very often in my husband's life, he referred to the time when he experienced his first fatality. It was in Lansing several months after he had joined the state police. The way he told it was that he had been called to an accident where a man—he referred to him as a Black minister—had been injured by a streetcar in Lansing. When he arrived, his impression was that the man had been cut in two—now, he was not exactly cut in two, but the accident was quite violent. He also had to go to the home of the victim and break the terrible news to his wife and take her to the hospital to see her husband.

Florentine Baril

The night that my father died I went and saw his body not too long after they had brought it into the funeral home. While my mother was talking, I slipped into the back where they had the body on the table, and I saw what had happened. The streetcar had cut him just below the torso and it had cut his left leg completely off and had crushed the right leg, because the streetcar had . . . had just run right over him. He ended up bleeding to death.

My mother never really got a chance to talk to him and find out what it is that he wanted to pass on to her before he died. This had a devastating effect upon her.

Wilfred Little

Relief food, distributed all over the country during the Depression, 1930s.

Here all of a sudden, here's a lady that's in her mid-thirties, with a house full o' children, and her husband's gone. It's just like you have to start everything out from scratch.

Wilfred Little

We used to buy a hundred-pound bag of day-old bread for five cents at Old Castle's Bakery in Lansing. But that day-old bread actually was about a month old. My mother knew how to fix it—she would take it and cut off the mold and put sugar on it and put it in the oven and soften it with water. We ate like it was the last supper.

Abdul Aziz Omar

My mother never did like to accept welfare. This was the hardest thing that she had to deal with after my father's death. This put them into her business, which she just didn't like.

Wilfred Little

My mother had a lot of pride. She sewed. She crocheted gloves for people. She did a lot of things, not to be dependent solely on welfare. She rented out garden space, she sharecropped with the men that would come and rent garden space. We had a dump behind our house; she rented that out. So she knew how to make money. And she never developed a welfare mentality.

Yvonne Woodward

After my father got killed, we got looser and looser. Malcolm and I were full of mischief. Young boys just coming along, just finding out how far we could spit, really. And all of our acquaintances and associates were white people—white boys. They had the nerve to not go home from school or to go home and then come back over to our house to create mischief. We didn't have that kind of nerve, you know—we had been trained to stay in our own yard and to hoe in the garden and all this. Well, we weren't as punctual in hoeing the garden as we had started out with my father.

Abdul Aziz Omar

Talking about Malcolm and Philbert, a story comes to mind about how, as my father would put it, *mysterious* they were, always lookin' for tricks to play on somebody, including me, if they ever had the chance. I can remember one of their neighbors, who was sorta feisty, and who used to give them a bad time every now and then. At Halloween, they decided to play this trick on him. They went out and moved his outhouse—everybody had outhouses then. Then they stayed around long enough for him to know that they were out there doing something. When he came out to chase them, all of a sudden he just dropped out of sight with a scream and fell into the hole that they had prepared as they moved the outhouse.

Cyril McGuire

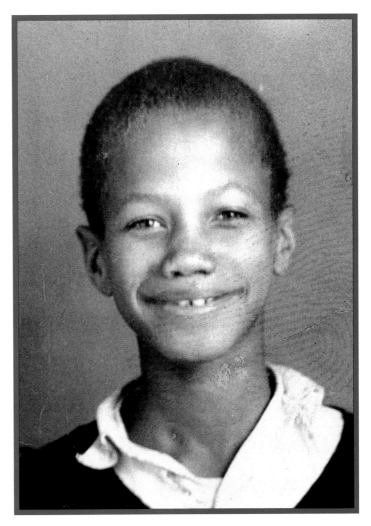

Young Malcolm, 1930s.

Our mother would send the three of us out in the fields to work. Malcolm would start talking, and we would start working. I've thought about this over the years—I can remember Malcolm laying under a tree with a straw in his mouth. Malcolm was telling these stories, but we were so happy to be around him that we worked—and Malcolm was using psychology, and we didn't realize it.

Yvonne Woodward

Malcolm liked to play. When a group would start playing, he would end up being the one that was leading the group. Now, we were the only Black children in the neighborhood, but on the back of our property we had a wooded area, so the white kids would all come over to our house, and they'd go back and play in the woods. So Malcolm would say, "Let's go play Robin Hood." Well, we'd go back there, and Robin Hood was Malcolm. And these white kids would go along with it—a Black Robin Hood.

Wilfred Little

We had a dog that somebody shot. It was just one thing after another. They shot this dog just for the purpose of seeing to it that you don't have a dog, I guess, just to give you a hard time. When they would come to the house, they would speak to my mother in a way where they were trying to get her to kneel, you know, because she was independent, and she didn't feel that she had to go through all these changes that they wanted—"If you want this check, you're going to do this or that." That's what they continuously were working at, was breaking her spirit.

Wilfred Little

Wesley, Yvonne, and Reginald, Malcolm's younger siblings, in front of their Lansing home, 1930s.

I remember when the welfare authorities would come—this lady in this little black hat, they always wore black. My mother would send us off into the fields or send us out to play, because apparently she didn't want us to know what was happening. But she was always upset when they left. And I heard her accusing them of setting her up—she was always saying, "You know what you're doing to me." And I don't know what that was, other than she felt they were harassing her, they were doing something to her.

Yvonne Woodward

Nuns feed hungry children during the Depression, 1930s.

One day the Jerry Rowe Company—I'll call their name—came up to the house and took all of my mother's new bedroom furniture out. My mother kept saying, "I have paid this, I have the receipt." The man would not listen. They hauled all the furniture out of the house into this truck and took it away. The next day she went down there. Now, the neighbors saw all this furniture leave, right? Now, how many of them saw it come back? They didn't know that that furniture was paid for. The store apologized, but look what they put my mother through.

Yvonne Woodward

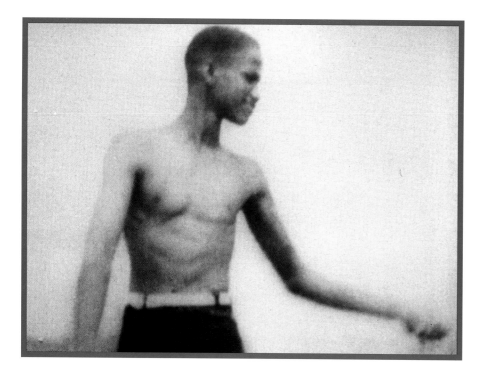

Malcolm at age fourteen, 1939.

Once Malcolm and his buddy were going through the woods, through the fields, and I wanted to go. They didn't want me to, so they started running—and I started running. I was keeping up pretty good, and Malcolm got mad at that, so he reached back and grabbed hold of my hand, and he said, "Okay, you wanna go, come on." And he pulled me, and my little legs were just stretching, trying to keep up with him. He intended for me to fall on my face—he was gonna drag me and teach me a lesson. But the fact that I kept up with him—his whole countenance changed. He was so happy and so proud that I could keep up with him that he kept on, and we ran, we ran and ran. And he started laughing, and from then on it was a game, he used to do that all the time.

Yvonne Woodward

At this time I was boxing; Malcolm didn't box. I would get up every morning, run a mile and walk a mile—that's what the man said I should do. Malcolm didn't do that, because Malcolm was not too successful at boxing. So to balance this out, Malcolm began to go down into Lansing; he got in contact with the westsiders, the African Americans, and they'd play around.

At that time Lincoln Community Center was just being established. There was a lady by the name of Mrs. Majors that was in charge, and Malcolm kept getting into trouble with Mrs. Majors. She didn't like Malcolm because he was so forthright; you see, he would talk back to her and all this, and naturally that upset her and she wanted to subdue him. They kept getting into it, so finally she called the police and they got after Malcolm. Malcolm went and hit Mrs. Majors with his fist in her rump—she was about four feet across.

Abdul Aziz Omar

Joe Louis knocks out Max Schmeling, June 23, 1938.

Harlemites celebrate a Louis victory, 1936.

My mother had been a widow for seven years when a nice man came on the scene, and she was real happy, she glowed. He was a very nice man. After a while the visits stopped, and it became evident that she was pregnant. She lost her glow.

Yvonne Woodward

How is a woman that's got seven children gonna get married? Who's gon' marry a woman with seven children—they can fall in love with her, yeah, but who's gon' marry her?

Wilfred Little

A physician's certification of Louise Little's condition, signed January 3, 1939.

PHYSICIAN'S CERTIFICATE—Mentally Diseased, Laws of 1923.   9505 (1923 Rev.)   4 3R5a→

PROBATE JUDGES   DOUBLEDAY BROS & CO LAW BLANK Makers

State of Michigan,

The Probate Court for the County of Ingham

In the Matter of Louise Little

Insane

COUNTY OF Ingham ,) ss.

I, Dr. E.F. Hoffman , do hereby certify that I am a permanent resident of the City of Mason , in said County, and a graduate of Rush Medical College, University of Chicago , an incorporated medical college; that I am registered according to law, and have practiced as a physician 3½ years; that, acting under the direction and by the appointment of said Court, I did on the 3rd day of January A. D. 19 39 personally examine said Louise Little

I further certify that in my opinion said Louise Little is a n insane person and her condition is such as to require care and treatment in an institution for the care, custody and treatment of such mentally diseased persons, and that the facts and circumstances upon which such opinion is based, are as follows:

Female Department Michigan Insane Asylum

Louise Little remained in the mental institution at Kalamazoo for over twenty-five years.

Kalamazoo was one of the state institutions for people who had mental problems. It was like this great big campus with all these various buildings on it. When I would go to see my mother—I tried to go every two weeks—at first she had a time trying to adjust to all these conditions that existed, because there were some people there that needed to be there. But after a while she began to resign herself to her fate, as she would say.

Wilfred Little

Being torn apart from my family at nine, when we'd always been very tight, was painful. But I don't think I ever shed tears. I put on a strong front. The tears were inside, because I can remember being petrified. I didn't know how to live around anyone else. I don't think any of my family ever dealt with the others' and their own pain. You're suddenly spread apart, and I know that they have feelings, but to this day we have never gotten together and talked about our pain. I know how strong it was. And I know that they had it.

Yvonne Woodward

The Little family had a dignity. When you think of how difficult it was for them, yet they didn't expect any sympathies, nor did they act like they should get it. They probably had had a rough time, but you'd never know it. I certainly was proud to call them my friends.

Jenny Washington

When we'd go visit my mother, she would beg us to get her outta there because, she said, "They're going to take my land." The land that we were on was very important to my mother. It was important to us that our father and mother bought it. My father built that home, and my mother always said she loved that tract of land. And it was a desirable piece. The taking of the land was traumatic to us.

Yvonne Woodward

When Malcolm went to Mason, you could see a change in him. Some for the better, some for the worse. After a while he started feeling somewhat at home. Sometimes he would complain about some of the things the teachers would try to do—they would try to discourage him from taking courses that Black people weren't supposed to take; in other words, keep him in his place.

Wilfred Little

I think often he probably was frustrated because we didn't know anything about the social problems of a Black person. We were very naive, and the world was all small-townish. You know. And I think I can remember times when I sensed that he was frustrated with just the differences.

Belva Cotton

In 1940 Malcolm played football for Mason High School. A local newspaper story recalls his past, 1960s.

X MARKS MALCOLM X-- Back in 1940 Malcolm X, or Malcolm Little as he was known then, showed a preference for tackling ball carriers for good old Mason High instead of tackling the white race as he is doing today. Malcolm X is one of the most controversial and, in some quarters, feared

Well, Malcolm did make a tremendous impact on Mason in the junior high school when he came in, because he was such a dynamic individual. He was a great leader. He had a natural ability for leadership. Yet he had a great humility about him as he did this. It wasn't a backing down or a cowardice in any way. I didn't ever feel he was arrogant.

Jim Cotton

There in Mason, Malcolm seemed to fit the mold and, I would say, go along with the process. As I recall him in Lansing, in junior high school, as a matter of fact, he seemed to be more in a belligerent mood, or an angry mood. A defiant mood—seeking attention, probably.

Cyril McGuire

Malcolm leaves for Boston, 1940: posing, *center*, with Yvonne and Reginald, and, *bottom*, with Yvonne, *far left*, Reginald and neighbors.

I said Malcolm's got a home with me as long as I got a home. Sittin' there with his hand in his mouth, he said, "I'm going to Boston, I'm going to Boston with my big sister." He gets up and dances around the room — he's going to Boston!

Ella Collins

FROM
CRIME TO
CONSCIOUSNESS

By 1941, Ella had negotiated with the Michigan authorities to gain custody of Malcolm. She sent for him to come live with her, his half brother, Earl, Jr., and his half sister Mary in Ella's house on "the Hill" in Roxbury. Malcolm arrived but quickly deserted "the Hill" for the swinging nightlife "downtown," plunging wholeheartedly into the swirling, dancing,

Malcolm in a mug shot at the time
of his arrest, 1946.

hustling, hair-conking, zoot-suit-wearing, woman-chasing, reefer-smoking fast life of Black Boston. He worked a variety of odd jobs, as shoeshine boy, busboy, soda jerk, factory and shipyard worker, but his heart was in learning the hustler's craft, which was fast becoming his real profession. Soon Boston wasn't big enough for Malcolm. After less than a year, he hit the road to the hustler's capital, New York.

For the next four years, Malcolm was on the move, shuttling between New York, Boston, and Michigan. He worked in a jewelry store, on the railroad, in a defense plant, and he waited tables in Small's Paradise in Harlem, while descending ever deeper into the criminal netherworld. He dealt drugs and pimped; he stuck people up and became a burglar. Except for his ties to his brother Reginald, who lived with him for a time, he seems to have lost all family and moral mooring. On a trip to Boston he steals his aunt's fur coat. In Detroit he robs a friend. He has become a predator without a conscience.

Occasionally flashes of pseudoracial consciousness break through, as in 1942 when he receives his draft notice and goes around Harlem saying that he wants "to fight for the Japanese and kill crackers." This was undoubtedly hype for Malcolm (it got him rejected as "a psychopathic personality"). But back home in Michigan, Elijah Muhammad, who would soon help rescue Malcolm from the darkness into which he had fallen, was doing real time in prison for counseling Black men to resist the draft and not fight "our Asiatic brother."

Race politics, however, was actually the farthest thing from Malcolm's mind. He had run afoul of the Harlem numbers runner West Indian Archie and had to return to Boston to avoid being killed. He resumed a relationship with a white woman with whom he had been consorting off and on for years, and together with her friends, they formed an interracial burglary ring, which operated out of an apartment in Harvard Square.

At first they did quite well. But Malcolm eventually got caught trying to recover stolen property from a pawnshop. The white women turned state's evidence, got probation and a suspended sentence, and

Malcolm's lover served seven months. Malcolm, on the other hand, received a ten-year sentence—in large part, he believed, because the authorities frowned upon his forbidden relations with the women. (Unbeknownst to Malcolm, he had dodged a more crippling racist bullet when the women, to their credit, resisted police overtures that they accuse Malcolm and his confederates of rape.)

He was sent to Charlestown Prison. The year was 1946, and he was not yet twenty-one years old.

PRISONER (1946–52)

The Horatio Alger dimension of Malcolm's transformation in prison, his phoenix-like rise from the ashes of degradation, has added considerably to his legend. Yet in focusing on Malcolm's individual conversion to Islam, we overlook the appeal of Islam to Blacks in general; we overlook the role of human encouragement, which played so significant a part in his self-reappraisal; we overlook the role of his family in recruiting him; and we overlook the damage of racism, which placed Malcolm on the path to nihilism in the first place.

First came the human support he got from his role model in prison, "Bimbi," who was regarded as the smartest convict in the prison and who got respect not with violence or bluster but "with words." It was Bimbi who told Malcolm that he had a mind, if he would only develop it.

It was such a small thing, just a little human encouragement, but it contrasted sharply with his Mason teachers, who had denigrated his achievements and consigned Malcolm, apparently forever, to life as an American outcast (a role he acted out rather well).

Having been awakened to the possibility of new personal growth by Bimbi, Malcolm is approached by his siblings, who want him to join them in their new religion, Islam. Consequently, when Malcolm does join the Nation, he is simply the latest member of his family to do so. Wilfred and Hilda, who helped raise him, were already members, as were

Philbert and Reginald, a younger brother with whom he was closest during his hustling days. On one level, then, Malcolm's conversion may be viewed as an act of renewing family ties cut off by personal tragedy or, in Malcolm's case, individual waywardness. It was also a reconnection with those days when their mother read to them from *The Negro World* and their father spoke to them of "the great race work" to be done.

This family history is important because it links Malcolm's individual conversion to the larger social allure of Muhammad's teachings, which impacted on four individuals who had gone their separate ways yet came to common agreement on the nature of racial oppression in America. Seen in this light, the responsibility for Malcolm's conversion is not primarily Malcolm's or Muhammad's or Bimbi's or his siblings'. It is the American denial of human recognition to Blacks that alienated Malcolm—and alienates untold numbers today.

We cannot, however, discount the indisputable importance of Elijah Muhammad's role in Malcolm's conversion, because Muhammad's human sensitivity in reaching out to Malcolm made Malcolm feel a vital part of his new religious-political family. Himself incarcerated by the FBI for sedition, conspiracy, and violation of the draft laws, Muhammad could understand the psyche of a fellow Black convict. He wrote and sent money to Malcolm, who was a perfect stranger. Again were wonders wrought by a little human kindness.

All these forces combined to crack the dam of Malcolm's stunted intellectual development and allow his prodigious natural talent to burst through. Piece by piece, he refined a method of intellectual development that made him one of the great critical thinkers of his or any time.

CONVERT

The first step was honest self-criticism. Malcolm freely faced up to his faults. His reading comprehension had deteriorated. He practiced writing the alphabet over and over again until his handwriting improved. To cure his ignorance, he embarked on what we might call the "dictionary project," a systematic study from *a* to *z*. The dictionary revived his old love for history and gave him a new interest: philology. But philology is more than a study of words; it is a form of applied logic. And Malcolm was a logician. That's why he loved debating. He liked constructing logical arguments regardless of what side he was on. He used to try to anticipate what the other side might say and prepare responses. Examining both sides of an issue for the purpose of improving one's own argument is intellectual rigor of a high order, and that was a key element of Malcolm's approach: systematic study and reflection.

Then there was history. He had always loved it, but now he had a purpose: to verify the religious-historical claims of the Nation of Islam. So he dove into the books in his typical way: with everything that was in him. He became a *student*, a near-obsessed student, who kept reading long after the prison lights went out and eventually developed astigmatism. But that was Malcolm's way. Whatever he was into, he was into totally.

Malcolm also had genuine intellectual curiosity. As driven as he was to acquire knowledge to expose the crimes of the white West, he would pause sometimes for pure intellectual enjoyment, examining a question that had nothing to do with race, such as the authorship of Shakespeare's plays: "No color was involved there; I just got intrigued over the Shakespearean dilemma."

I think we fail to perceive Malcolm as a true intellectual because we regard as intellectuals those who communicate via the written word and to a certain audience. But Malcolm's métier was the *spoken word*. Moreover, Malcolm tailored his teachings to his audience, whether one of academics, Christians, or folks from the street. He was intellectually flexible, because his first priority was *to communicate* in order to instruct. He spoke to people in the language they understood, because he was a people's intellectual, not an intellectual's intellectual.

(Why is it so difficult to recognize Malcolm as the prodigy he was?

Some of my Afrocentrist friends have asked why we take Plato's word that Socrates was a great thinker, though we have nothing that Socrates wrote. Why, then, is it so difficult to accept an African or American griot as a genuine intellect but so easy to accept a Greek one? Malcolm would have an answer for that, of course.)

And Malcolm was a voracious reader. He read everything. Once, I caught him reading the *National Review* and asked why he was reading that "right-wing garbage." And he said, "Because you never can tell where you'll come up with a good idea." Probing, inquiring mind? Malcolm X.

It was in prison, then, that Malcolm found his new identity and his calling. Motivated by Bimbi and Muhammad, he became a student and an unofficial minister. He now tutored other inmates, reenacting the path his parents had trod.

MALCOLM'S NEW FAMILY

Family was important in the life of Malcolm X as it is important in the life of us all. His nuclear family had fought valiantly to preserve itself against the ravages of a jealous racism and an abandoning economy. But when both parents became casualties of this war of racist political economy, and the children's struggle to keep things together could not hold back the tide of disintegration, the Black extended family in the person of Ella Collins intervened to rescue Malcolm at the edge of the engulfing wave. It is only when Malcolm deserts his biological family for the family of the streets that he becomes lost. And he is not "found" again until he reconnects with his family and, through them, connects with the larger racial family embodied in the Nation of Islam and its leader, the Honorable Elijah Muhammad.

That Malcolm loved Elijah Muhammad seems undeniable, for if deeds mirror devotion, no one could possibly have worked harder and therefore loved Elijah Muhammad more than Malcolm. Some have suggested that Malcolm joined the Nation primarily because he saw in Elijah Muhammad a surrogate father. It is true that there are striking similarities in the backgrounds of Earl Little and Elijah Muhammad in the sense that Elijah Muhammad, born in 1897, was, like Earl Little, from a small, racially stratified Georgia town. Like Earl Little, Elijah Muhammad was indifferently educated by what passed for the colored "school system" of those days, reaching only the fourth grade. Like Earl Little, Elijah Muhammad grew up to practice a churchless Baptist ministry alongside the jobs he took to support himself and his young family. And like Earl Little, and many thousands before him, Elijah Muhammad came to despair of ever leading a manly and entitled existence in Klan-run Georgia, so he, too, migrated north in search of the Great Black Dream of a better and a freer life.

Both men reacted to their racial experiences by turning to a religion that espoused a special destiny and purpose for the Black race as distinct from—and in opposition to—the white world. That doctrine was familiar to Malcolm and his siblings because they had absorbed it at their parents' knees. So their subsequent embrace of Elijah Muhammad's Islam seems both psychologically and ideologically natural. That is why reducing Malcolm's attraction to Elijah Muhammad to pseudo-Freudian speculations underestimates the political appeal of Muhammad's Manichaean vision of the world, a vision that drew its compelling force not from unconscious psychological drives but from the consciousness-raising experience of being racial underlings in America. It was the dehumanizing Black experience that drew most of the Little family—Wilfred, Hilda, Philbert, and Reginald—into the Nation before Malcolm, and it was that experience, codified into an anti-Christian, anti-white religion and philosophy, which would, in Malcolm's hands, draw in thousands, thousands more.

That was the potential Elijah Muhammad seems to have sensed in his new disciple. Here, at last, was the "son" for whom he had been seeking, the son with the drive and energy and dedication to build a new world in his, Muhammad's, name.

But Muhammad already had a family, and six biological sons. So where was this new one to fit? In a way that could not then be foreseen, the coming of Malcolm would raise within the Nation of Islam the most fundamental questions about the politics of religion and the religion of politics.

In 1952–53, however, those issues were all obscured, awaiting that future time when the Nation had become a prize, and an enterprise, worthy of the life-and-death struggle that would take place over its ownership, its direction, its process of succession.

In Their Own Words

Ella Collins	Malcolm's elder half sister
Alex Haley	Coauthor of *The Autobiography of Malcolm X*
Malcolm Jarvis	Close friend in Boston ("Shorty" in the autobiography) and fellow inmate in Charlestown and Norfolk prisons
Stanley Jones	Fellow inmate in Norfolk Prison Colony
Wilfred Little	Malcolm's eldest brother
Cyril McGuire	Childhood friend in Lansing
Imam Wallace D. Mohammed	Formerly known as Wallace D. Muhammad, son of Elijah Muhammad
Abdul Aziz Omar	Formerly Philbert Little, Malcolm's second elder brother
Yvonne Little Woodward	Malcolm's younger sister

Well, he was a type of person whose appearance would electrify you. Some people, you can sense them. You can feel them. And he was the type of person that when he walked down the street, you could sense and feel there was something going on with him.

Malcolm Jarvis

Malcolm at age fifteen, with his hair conked, Boston, 1941.

When Frank Sinatra used to sing, and bobby-sockers would swoon? This is what the Black girls up in Roxbury and in Boston did when they saw Malcolm. He was a very tall, attractive sort of a fellow. I don't know what it is, but some guys, they just attract women like this, and they marveled over him. They'd knock you out, *out*, knock you down in the street to get to him, just to shake his hand or something like that, you know. He used to change clothes once or twice a day—another thing that had the girls all in a tizzy. He couldn't walk down the street but to stop traffic with people all up and down Humboldt Avenue.

Malcolm Jarvis

Malcolm was beginning to realize what the life of the big city was like. And he started experimenting with all parts of it. He was fascinated by the nightclubs and theaters and the entertainers that he got to know—a lot of things that he never had seen or had a chance to be exposed to before. He started growing up fast.

Wilfred Little

Ads for two popular Boston nightspots, 1940s.

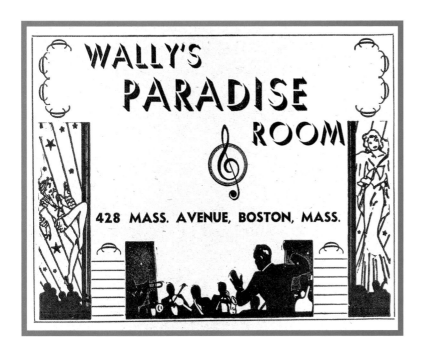

A couple dancing the lindy, 1940s.

Not long after arriving in Boston, Malcolm, posing with sister Ella, sports a zoot suit, 1940s.

Saturday night was the most exciting night of the week. Everybody was out drinking and having a good time, and around twelve o'clock, if you took a ride down Mass Avenue and parked, there were scenes of people half-drunk and the police knocking 'em and pushin' them around and arrestin' people. There was always a lot of action. That was the night when normal working-day citizens would catch the nightclub scene. They used to have a lot of name groups come in. All the Blacks from up in Roxbury used to hang out to the wee hours of the morning on Sunday.

Malcolm Jarvis

I remember him telling me with great seriousness about how he had learned his first hustle: that to be a shoeshine boy was okay. He would get, say, fifteen cents or maybe twenty cents per shine, but if he learned how to make the rag pop loudly—there was a way you could use the rag kind of loosely and then jerk it down on the shoe, and it would make a noise, a popping noise—people somehow liked that, and they would give Malcolm as much as a quarter tip. And so he became the poppingest shoeshine boy in town. And this type of thing, the hustler world, became part of him.

Alex Haley

The teenage Malcolm, 1940s.

Malcolm comes home in time for dinner, and he comes through the dining room door, popping his fingers and twisting his arms, singing "The St. Louis Blues," and heading for the kitchen. He's hungry, and you know it without question.

Ella Collins

With this particular suit on, he'd look like a man from Mars. He astonished all the girls and the fellows, too. When he was dancing, those pants were like he was a floating balloon. And that coat was like a wing, the way he'd be dancing and flying around with that big ten-gallon hat on and the chain flinging.

Malcolm Jarvis

Malcolm as a hipster in
Boston, age fifteen, 1941.

I remember when I went to Boston to visit Malcolm and my sister Ella, and when I caught up with him, he kept me strung out just like a child. I wasn't accustomed to just running from one place to another continuously. He took me by where he worked, we met a couple of the young girlfriends that he had and some cousins that I hadn't met. You could tell these were the people on the fast track. And that's what Malcolm was on.

Wilfred Little

Malcolm was a person that made friends easy, and he knew just about everybody. Whatever community he was in, it wouldn't be long before he would case that community out and know where everything was—good or bad. He was just very alert to people. And he could listen to a person speak, and after they'd leave he'd tell you what they really wanted to say.

Wilfred Little

Malcolm with Ella (*far right*) and friends at Franklin Park in Boston, 1940s.

Malcolm Jarvis at Wally's Paradise Room, Boston, 1943.

To him, actors or dancers or musicians, they were very exciting people. He just loved them. Something that he got from being around these type of people, I don't think I can find words to express it—it was like food is to a hungry body.

Malcolm Jarvis

As Malcolm got out onto the streets, even when he worked on the trains, he became aware of what's really going on out here in this world. He had reached a point where he said, "Hell, I never will make it, trying to be right. The only people that're really making it are the ones that's trying to do wrong. That includes the police department and the mayor and all them judges and all those people you see settin' up downtown handing us all this stuff." He said, "You'll never make it on these janitor jobs and selling sandwiches on these trains and shining shoes and stuff like that."

Wilfred Little

Railroad workers taking a break from kitchen dining car duties, 1940s.

When the white folks came out at night and wanted Black women, he could arrange for them to get 'em. If they wanted bootleg whiskey, if they wanted drugs, he knew where to get them. He would be in the middle where he could make a profit off of it.

Wilfred Little

The 369th in
training, upstate
New York, 1943.

A famous World
War II recruiting
poster.

Zoot suits, from
the everyday to
the extreme,
were in style,
1940s.

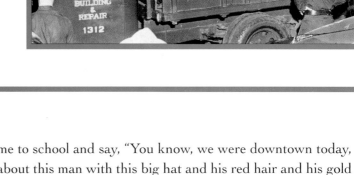

Aftermath of the 1943
Harlem riot.

In Lansing some kids would come to school and say, "You know, we were downtown today, and we saw this man." They'd tell about this man with this big hat and his red hair and his gold chain and these pants this wide, and I'd laugh. I'd say, "oh really." You see, I never told them that was my brother.

Yvonne Woodward

Malcolm was into marijuana in those days. He'd go to New York, I don't know where his connection was there, but he would come back with marijuana sewed into the lining of that big, heavy overcoat he used to wear. I've seen him take a needle and break the lining open and take the stuff out. Sometimes he had as much as a quarter to a half a pound of it, and then he would package it up himself, roll it up into joints and sell them for a dollar apiece.

Malcolm Jarvis

To Malcolm, white women had the money and the Black ones didn't. That's why his preference was, in those days, more to the white. They could afford to give him some of the things that he wanted and show him a good time. Now, he was very respectful of the Black women, I will say that. But he frequented the white ones because of that—money.

Malcolm Jarvis

One Saturday night when we were at the Savoy, Malcolm was sittin' at the table with this girl, Bea, and her sister, Joyce, and myself. Bea was in love with Malcolm. She had a puff, and Malcolm had his .32 under the table or some kind of way in his pocket, when the cops came in. He passed the gun to Bea, and she put the gun in her puff. Naturally, being that she was a white girl, the cops weren't gonna bother her. But they made Malcolm stand up and patted him down. He was clean, and they didn't say anything. But Bea—this'll show you how crazy she was— she had the gun out under the table. She said if they was gettin' ready to take him away, they would shoot. Gonna shoot the cop. Ha-ha-ha. You imagine that?

Malcolm Jarvis

Living the hustler's life as Big Red / Detroit Red, 1940s.

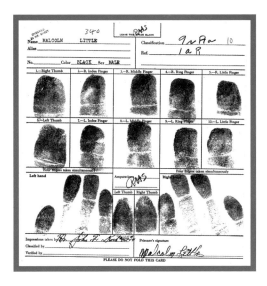

Malcolm's fingerprints, taken from his Detroit police record, 1940s.

A neighborhood and a famous entertainment spot that Malcolm knew in his Harlem days: St. Nicholas Avenue, looking north from 135th Street.

Billie Holiday with Apollo Theater photographer Gordon Anderson, 1950s.

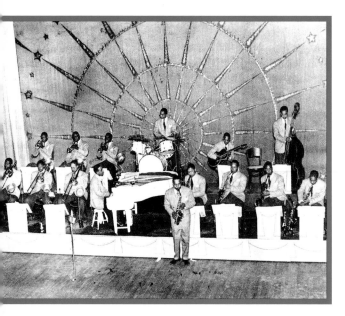

Benny Carter and his orchestra, appearing at the Apollo, 1942.

Malcolm had the reputation as being a hustler, and he was a streetwise person. But he was not a gangster in the sense that he would take a gun and hold people up, no. He carried a gun, but more or less for his own personal protection. The law looked at him, even the private detectives who used to ride around Roxbury in their cars out of station nine, they always kept an eye on him.

Malcolm Jarvis

He didn't have the temerity, I suppose you'd call it, to be bad. Malcolm was good. Everybody who knows Malcolm would tell you, he was a good man. And this is even before he came into Islam. He was not vulgar. And he was not disrespectful of your rights. He was a braggadocio. He would brag about what he had done and this and that, but it hadn't been that bad. He just knew how to tell it so it sounded as though he was a gang leader. But he didn't have no gang.

Abdul Aziz Omar

West Indian Archie was some kind of a numbers writer in New York, as far as I can remember. He's the one that Malcolm used to have to answer to when he was pickin' up numbers, and West Indian Archie had the direct contact with the Mafia, or whoever it was that was backin' the numbers. One night Malcolm was given the money by West Indian Archie to pay somebody off, and he didn't. It got back to Archie, and Archie reported it to the syndicate. There was a contract put out on Malcolm, who was staying at Sammy McKnight's house. Sammy called me up and said, "Jarvis, you better come and get your boy out of town." But when I drove down to New York, Sammy didn't know where he was. He said, "Right down on the corner, I think on Edgecombe and St. Nicholas Avenue, you might see him." Sure enough, he popped up. He didn't even take the time to go get his clothes, he was that shaky. He got in the car and said, "Jarvis, just the highway." And gone. He left his clothes and everything.

Malcolm Jarvis

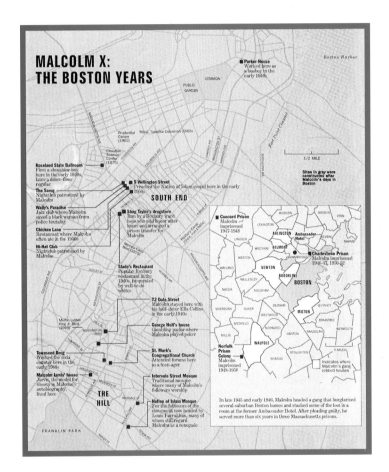

We were out at Bea's house partying and somebody suggested we go out and break into somebody's house again—we'd been in about four houses at that time. So we went out to Brookline, and I went into this house with Malcolm. To show you how fast Malcolm thinks, we were cruisin' down toward the West Roxbury highway, on the edge of Newton, and the police car was headin' for us. They would've caught us dead to right with all this stolen merchandise in the back of the car. So Malcolm says, "Back up and stop the car, and get out and ask which way is it back to Roxbury." So I stopped and asked the cop, "Sir, can you tell us how to get into Roxbury?" He says, "Well, where are you coming from?" And I told him we just came in from New York and got lost. So the cop says, "Well, you go this way and this way, and you're right into Roxbury." That's what saved us— Malcolm's quick wit of thinking to approach the cop before he approached us.

Malcolm Jarvis

They had a cage in the Middlesex County courtroom; they always brought the so-called prisoners out and locked them in this cage. Because the girls in the case were white, the detectives were all prejudiced. One comes out and says, "Well, if we had you niggers down south, we'd lynch you." When he said that, the blood rose to my head and Malcolm's head and both of us reached through the bars tryin' to grab the detective, but he just got out the way. We were already locked up and gonna go to jail anyway, so we would've tried to do him in right then and there.

Malcolm Jarvis

Well, I was what you call a mad Negro, I was one. And I knew what I saw was real. I know it wasn't anything funny about. I knew that when they'd laughed all together, they were laughin' like, "Look what we did. We doin' it to the Negro."

Ella Collins

Commonwealth of Massachusetts

MIDDLESEX, TO WIT:

At the SUPERIOR COURT, begun and holden at the City of Cambridge within and for the County of Middlesex, on the first Monday of February in the year of our Lord one thousand nine hundred and forty-six.

THE JURORS for the COMMONWEALTH OF MASSACHUSETTS on their oath present, that Beatrice Bazarian, Kora Marderosian, Malcolm Little, ~~Malcolm L. Jarvis~~ and Francis E. Brown on the eleventh day of December in the year of our Lord one thousand nine hundred and forty-five at Arlington, in the County of Middlesex aforesaid, in the nighttime did break and enter the dwelling house of Rollin W. Hoyt situated in said Arlington, with intent therein to commit larceny, and did steal certain jewelry, articles of wearing apparel, clocks and money of the amount and of the value of four dollars all of the value of more than one hundred dollars

of the property of Rollin W. Hoyt in said dwelling house.

Against the peace of said Commonwealth, and contrary to the form of the statute in such case made and provided.

Details of two of the larceny counts against Malcolm and his codefendants, February 1, 1946.

Malcolm's request for permission to appeal his eight-to-ten-year sentence, February 28, 1946.

Commonwealth of Massachusetts

MIDDLESEX, SS.
~~SUFFOLK~~, SS.
No. 3175 3-4-5-6

SUPERIOR COURT

COMMONWEALTH
v.
MALCOLM LITTLE

REQUEST FOR LEAVE TO APPEAL

To the Hon. Allen G. Buttrick Justice of the Superior Court.

Respectfully represents said defendant that on February 27, 1946 he was sentenced by you in said court sitting within and for the county of Suffolk, to the State Prison for the term of not more than Ten years and not less than eight years and that being aggrieved thereby he requests leave to appeal to the Appellate Division of said court for a review of said sentence s.

Malcolm Little
(Signature of Defendant)

Feb 28 1946

NOTE: The time within which this request may be filed is 3 days after the date of the imposition of a sentence.

A view of Concord Reformatory, 1940s.

A Charlestown Prison cellblock, 1945.

Charlestown was built basically out of granite blocks, and the prison cells were damp, very wet, and they had lice crawling around. In warm weather the stone would sweat. All you had in this little cell was a cot, a bucket, and a washbasin, all right? They didn't have toilets in there. You had to use the bucket, and every time you went to use it, you lifted the cover off. Bein' so many weeks or months old, the odor would knock you down, just like a poison gas. But you had to stomach it. If you had just gotten through eating, you would put your food all in the bucket. That's how bad it was. And bein' locked up seventeen to eighteen hours a day, that was enough to drive anybody crazy.

Malcolm Jarvis

Prison brought Malcolm to a standstill, and then he had to start taking a look at himself in comparison to this world that we live in out here, and just make a decision as to what he was going to do to be able to make it.

Wilfred Little

Malcolm vividly described prison life, that he was lonely, and limited. But he had plans to do a lot of reading. And he certainly did a lot of writing, because I think there were times when he probably wrote to me every week.

Cyril McGuire

Malcolm's brothers (*left to right*), Philbert, Wesley, Wilfred, and Reginald, 1949.

Temple of Islam members attend a federal hearing on sedition charges against three of their leaders, Chicago, 1942.

He wrote to me in the latter part of his prison experience, but when he first got in there, he didn't write. In fact, I learned that he was kind of a hell-raiser in prison, because he was trying to organize the people as though he was gon' break out and all this kind of stuff.

Abdul Aziz Omar

I came into the Muslim movement in 1947 and started bringing my brothers and sisters in. We already had been indoctrinated with Marcus Garvey's philosophy, so that was just a good place for us. They didn't have to convince us we were Black and should be proud or anything like that.

Wilfred Little

We all got together and decided we better let Malcolm know about this. Even though we had been scattered, we kept up with each other, and we tried to do things together as a family.

Wilfred Little

So I wrote to Malcolm and told him if he would believe in Allah that he would get out of prison. And that's all I wrote, because I knew he had very low tolerance for religion.

Abdul Aziz Omar

Before the Honorable Elijah Muhammad's release from prison, we were very much like any very private spiritualist religious movement. Upon his release he changed our focus from the lessons of the Nation of Islam to doing something practical to change our environment for the better. We lived mostly, and our temples were mostly located, in the worst parts of the African American environment. He wanted to see us move into better facilities, and he did it. Eight twenty-four East Forty-third Street was the first decent place that I know of for our meetings. Believe it or not, it was an animal hospital or dog pound, like, and the smell was there. But he had the courage to send the brothers in there. They cleaned the place up, and it was so attractive that when he moved to the next place, he was able to sell it to a preacher for a church.

Imam Wallace D. Mohammed

Elijah Muhammad, probably around the time of his wartime incarceration, 1940s.

I had completed my education I never would have been in prison today. I'm serving ten years for burglary on my first offense — my first crime. That doesn't hurt so because, being a Negro, I'm used to heavier punishment than usual But, I have long ago realized my mistakes and cannot see how an educated man would break into other peoples' houses.

Since my confinement I've already received a diploma in Elementary Eng lish through the State Correspondence Courses. I'm very much dissatisfied, though. There are many things that I would like to learn that would be of use to me when I regain my freedom. I do know that if I prepare myself now, while I have the time, I will never have to break the law to se-cure a living. It does hurt, tho', to watch murders, thieves with records dating back to the cradle, and "what not" going to Norfolk every day, while I (for reasons unknown to me) want to benefit by the place and can't get there for nothing.

I've been confined for eighteen months now and my record is clean. I've been here in Concord under Mr. O'Grady for six months and can only refer you to him for any reference of my character.

All I'm asking you for is a chance to amend my mistakes. Then, if I fail, I have no one to hate but myself

Thank You Kindly

Malcolm Little

In a letter from Concord prison, Malcolm pleads his case for transfer to Norfolk Prison Colony, July 28, 1947.

They would show you that all the hell the dark world is catching, they're getting it at the hands of the white man. So you don't have to die to go to hell, you can catch hell while you're living. And the white man is the one that's putting that hell on you. Well, that's a very convincing teaching, especially when you're using the white man's history to corroborate this.

Wilfred Little

Malcolm and I couldn't believe that society had put us away the way they had, and we were just two people that were out to rebel against it. In our own way. Now the only way we knew how to rebel was to cram some knowledge into our brains, so when we went back to society we wouldn't have to worry about ever going back to prison—because we'd know too much and be too smart for that.

Malcolm Jarvis

The Koran.

Malcolm and I were playing the part of, like, Solomon in the Bible—we were seeking knowledge and wisdom of the world. That's what had us going into these books on Egyptology, hieroglyphics, psychiatry, psychology, theology. We studied Shintoism, we studied many things out of these books that we had at the library. We were just seeking basic knowledge of what makes the world tick. We were trying to acclimate our minds into thinking on a much higher level than that of the average person.

Malcolm Jarvis

The Muslims were so strong about the pork, they wouldn't even get it for you on the chow line. It caused problems sometimes, because a lot of brothers couldn't understand, you know, why you won't get the pork for me. "You don't have to eat it, don't put it on your tray, just tell 'em to put it on my tray."

Stanley Jones

Malcolm always wrote about the righteousness of the world, and the goodness and purity of heart that a person should advocate in life. And all this knowledge was really coming out of the books that we had been reading, and when he started getting into racial things, and started putting it in these letters, you see, they used to casework your letters, and he had a casework record that high, just from letters that he wrote out of the prison. That's how they learned what our intentions were and what we were learning.

Malcolm Jarvis

Inmates walking the circle at Charlestown Prison, 1940s.

December 13, 1950

In the Holy Name of Allah, the True and Living God. And in the Name of His most humble Servant, the Honorable Mr. Elijah Mohammed.

As Salaam Alaikum

Commissioner MacDowell,

With america presently facing the most crucial crisis in her history, and the ultimate outcome of her plight depending solely upon her success in convincing The People of the East that she is truly seeking Peace, and that her aim, as she claims, is to guarntee the God-given Rights of all people...... despite race, creed or color...... This situation which now confronts the Muslims here at Charlestown must be brought to your attention.

We, being to all appearances such a small and isolated group, in comparisom to the Whole Body of Islam, the "uninformed" occidental mind would hastily, but unwisely, skoff at our importance, in so far as the present international situation is concerned. However, the more "fertile" minds of the occident would first take into consideration the important fact that the "fire" which "burned" Rome

Opening of a letter from Malcolm to Elliott MacDowell, Commissioner of Corrections, December 13, 1950.

The Muslims demanded respect and they got respect, and I think that was the important thing in any prison population. But the administration was more scared of 'em than anybody else.

Stanley Jones

We were taking these books out of the library, I'd say from nine months to a year before the prison got wise to it. And then they confiscated those books, took every one of 'em out of the library.

Malcolm Jarvis

I don't care what side of a debate Malcolm was on, he did an excellent job. The way he used to talk, he got a standing ovation, all the time. People listened—the issue was not whether they bought what he said or not; the fact was, he was able to get people's attention.

Stanley Jones

They would be debating different things on race, religion, and Malcolm would back 'em to the wall with his questions and answers. And then while he was talking, I would be jotting down questions. I'd be jotting down a rebuttal and shove it under under his hand, and he'd look down, and then he'd take over.

Malcolm Jarvis

Roxbury, 1952, an area where Malcolm would soon spur dramatic growth of the Nation of Islam.

Malcolm gave other inmates something to do, something to think about. Things to do that they would remember, to make them a better person on the outside.

Malcolm Jarvis

When Malcolm came out, he was full o' fire. He'd gotten so full o' fire that he got out at the right time and the right place, so he could expound. He came to Detroit, and he was surprised to find that there were so few people in this powerful teaching. He got on the podium, and he told them, "I'm ashamed, I'm surprised that you are sitting here, and so many empty seats." He said, "Every time you come out here, this place should be full." And that excited the Honorable Elijah Muhammad, it excited the believers who had any energy. And we brought in people, just hundreds of them.

Abdul Aziz Omar

After getting acquainted with him, observing him, I took a liking to him, like most of the young men of the Temple of Islam did. We were attracted to Malcolm. He automatically became like a leader for us, a role model. He was an inspiration, a great inspiration for the young men and boys of the Nation of Islam.

Imam Wallace D. Mohammed

The Honorable Elijah Muhammad would tell the ministers, "You have to be like Malcolm." He says, "Talk what the people understand. Talk about the things they know of, that are happening in their life."

Imam Wallace D. Mohammed

The Honorable Elijah Muhammad was teaching us that our place was not to fight the Caucasian—leave them alone. Just give 'em back everything they gave you, like whiskey, wine, beer, and learn how to take care of your own homes, your own family. And he said, "You don't have to touch them, Allah will destroy them. Allah will destroy the devil." In fact, he had to admonish Malcolm many times, because Malcolm, when he really got going, you'd have thought he had an army in the backroom to come and get you

Abdul Aziz Omar

Pickets outside the African consulate building,
Madison Avenue, New York City, 1952.

Malcolm X, probably early 1950s.

Now, my opinion of Malcolm's attitude from the days I knew him in prison and at the time I saw him in Boston after prison—he was a very cool, calm, and collected individual. In fact, it worried me, personally, that he was so quiet. Because you know, they say underneath all the calm is the storm. And his storm came later, as you all know.

Malcolm Jarvis

GROWING
AND OUTGROWING
THE NATION

MALCOLM: THE MASTER BUILDER

Some sense of Malcolm's centrality to the Nation of Islam's development may be gained by recalling that when its founder, W. D. Fard, disappeared in 1934, the Nation had one temple. In the years that followed, Elijah Muhammad enlarged the Nation to two viable temples, in Detroit and

Elijah Muhammad and Malcolm X, 1961.

Chicago, and two lesser ones, in Milwaukee and Washington—but the number of "believers" was counted only in the hundreds.

That was the situation in August 1952, when Malcolm was released from prison, having served six and a half years of his ten-year sentence. He spent one night with Ella in Boston and then went to Detroit, to stay with his brother Wilfred and join Detroit's Temple No. 1. Dismayed that Elijah Muhammad's message was not reaching larger numbers, Malcolm asked Elijah Muhammad at their first meeting, on Labor Day in Chicago, what he could do to spread the Word. Elijah Muhammad told him: "Go after the young people." Malcolm turned to the task with typical gusto. Despite working a full-time job and attending the three obligatory temple meetings each week, Malcolm went out after work to "fish" for recruits. In less than a year, he had tripled the membership of the Detroit temple and was made assistant minister.

Recognizing Malcolm's gift, Elijah Muhammad took him into his home in Chicago, to train him personally. Then, after months of tutelage, Malcolm was sent on his first trial run, to Flint and Lansing in his home state of Michigan. Passing that test successfully, he was next dispatched, in 1953, to another "home" territory, Boston, where he pulled together the nucleus that would develop into Muhammad's Temple No. 11.

In time, when the temple was solidly on its feet, Malcolm would turn it over to one of his brightest protégés, the multitalented Caribbean-born calypso singer, Gene Walcott, who performed professionally in his pre-Muslim days as "The Charmer." When he entered the Nation, Walcott reverted to his first name and became Louis X. Today he bears the honorific name bestowed upon him by Elijah Muhammad: Louis Farrakhan. But in this early period, it was "Brother Malcolm" and "Brother Louis," "homeboys" in the faith, bound together, like older and younger brother, in the new crusade.

Wherever Malcolm went, new temples sprang up and old ones increased their membership. He himself, downplaying the critical importance of his role, said: "I think I have had a hand in most of Mr. Muhammad's temples." As a reward, the Messenger, in June 1954, only a few weeks after the Supreme Court outlawed segregation in the public schools, made Malcolm minister of Temple No. 7, in Harlem.

Malcolm was on fire with the challenge of that appointment: "I can't start to describe for you my welter of emotions. For Mr. Muhammad's teachings really to resurrect American Black people, Islam obviously had to grow, to grow very big. And nowhere in America was such a single Temple potential available as in New York's five boroughs. . . . They contained over a million Black people."

In Washington, the white capital had spoken, renewing its pledge to solve the American race problem by its own methods, in its own way, and in its own time. Muhammad responded by sending Malcolm, his most brilliant and impatient disciple, into Harlem to win over the Black capital and its outlying provinces to the Muslim rejectionist point of view.

The contest was both symbolic and curiously American, pitting as it did the individual against the power of the state. Malcolm, however, was no ordinary individual. Renting a room in Queens, he set out on his unequal task.

Reviewing his schedule even now, years later, it seems superhuman, impossible. Malcolm was simultaneously the chief minister in New York, Philadelphia, and Boston. Traveling by bus and train (the Nation did not provide him with a car until 1956), Malcolm taught in Philadelphia on Wednesdays and Hartford on Thursdays, while fulfilling his regular duties in the New York temple. For the remainder of 1954 through 1955, he also pioneered temples in Springfield, Massachusetts, in Buffalo, Pittsburgh, Atlantic City, Newark, and Miami. His strategy seemed to be to consolidate an East Coast axis, but he also made exploratory forays into the South and Midwest, in Richmond and Cleveland. On paper it may not sound like much, but when we stop to calculate what was involved, Malcolm's achievements seem nothing less than miraculous.

Consider this: When Malcolm received his "new Chevrolet" in 1956, he put thirty thousand miles on it in five months—which means that he averaged two hundred miles a day, consistently and unfailingly, just going about his basic duties! His other leadership responsibilities—organizing, nurturing, administering, innovating, proselytizing, pastoring, and self-educating—he had to find time for on top of the travel. When we add to this load the fact that he seems also to have visited Chicago at least once a month to report to Mr. Muhammad, and to bring him the monthly collection, not to mention his writing reports to Chicago in the interim, we can begin to get a sense of how Herculean Malcolm's labors were.

The fruits of those labors were self-evident: By 1957, there were twenty-seven temples. By 1959, there were forty-nine, "an unknown number of smaller missions," and an estimated forty thousand members and untold sympathizers.

It was a long way from 1952 and the gathering of a few hundred where a newly released prisoner from Massachusetts had, somewhat timidly, asked the Honorable Elijah Muhammad: "What can I do to help?"

The measure of Malcolm is that virtually single-handedly, and in a few short years, he had done what Elijah Muhammad and W. D. Fard had been unable to do. He had done more than any of Muhammad's sons or any of his ministers. He had built the Nation.

MALCOLM'S EXCEPTIONALITY

We have been cautioned during the recent Malcolm renaissance not to romanticize Malcolm, not to make him bigger than life, to remember, after all, that he was a mortal being. This has always struck me as a curious admonition, coming as it does from a society that reveres so many with so little cause. But in Malcolm's case, we need not argue subjectively about his uniqueness or his greatness. For in the annals of American history, only a handful of men have demonstrated the ability to inspire a mass movement on the basis of their personality and charisma alone, and then exhibited the organizational intelligence to institutionalize that movement so that it outlived them.

There was Martin Luther King. But even Martin forged a coalition of *existing* churches into the Southern Christian Leadership Conference, whereas Malcolm had to build his "churches" from scratch and then structure them into the Nation's framework. There was Marcus Garvey, who arrived in America in 1916 seeking to emulate Booker T. Washington and was radicalized by white America into constructing the greatest international Black movement of all time. There was Elijah Muhammad, whose vision Malcolm made whole. And there was Cesar Chavez, who, in the sixties, "went from door to door in the barrios where the farm workers lived" to build the United Farm Workers Union in California.

Black, brown, or white, I can think of no others.

There is still another context in which to evaluate Malcolm's significance, the context of fate and history. Reflecting on the incomparable Haitian leader, Toussaint L'Ouverture, in *The Black Jacobins*, his seminal work on the Haitian revolution, the West Indian intellectual C. L. R. James, quite the fabulous individual himself, wrote: "Men make history but only so much history as it is possible for them to make." This was as true of Malcolm as it was of Toussaint. They made history, but history also made them.

One of the reasons Malcolm was able to make history is that he was an independent and creative thinker, always ready to test his theories in action. Sitting those first weeks in Temple No. 1 in Detroit, for example, still only a novice in the faith, he regarded the sparse attendance as an insult. He therefore "disagreed" with the "self-defeating waiting view . . . that Allah would bring us more Muslims. . . . I thought we should go out into the streets and get more Muslims into the fold." So one key to Malcolm's success was that he brought a new methodology and a new recruiting psychology into the Nation.

He was also totally dedicated to whatever he was committed to, an example being his prodigious prison study, where he read as much as fifteen hours a day in pursuit of the "new knowledge."

His capacity to follow through on his commitments was based on his sense of discipline and was reflected in his concern for time and his habit of always being on time. This disciplined approach to life manifested itself as well in the personal regimen that allowed him to function effectively—for years—on one meal a day and four hours' sleep. (His brother Philbert maintained that even as a boy, Malcolm had an amazing energy level that made it almost impossible to keep up with him.)

Then there was his attention to organizational details and his unceasing effort to improve himself and his effectiveness. He was never without a notebook in which he jotted down appointments and ideas and points to look into further as intellectual grist to feed his ever-churning mind.

Malcolm also had considerable interpersonal skills. He was thoughtful, accessible, receptive, and courteous—even when he was giving the "devils" hell. His receptivity could be seen in the myriad phone calls he made—and accepted—from friends and strangers, and his thoughtfulness was manifested in little acts like picking up Alex Haley at the airport and chauffeuring him home. And this with Malcolm's schedule!

The fact that he found time for these generous acts not as public gestures but as private rituals of friendship is a key to what set Malcolm apart from so many self-important and self-designated leaders of our time.

Writer-poet Sonia Sanchez, then an activist with the Congress of Racial Equality (CORE), told of encountering Malcolm as he gave a speech in Harlem one afternoon and standing for hours, even after it began raining, to listen. When Malcolm finished, she went up to him to tell him how much she liked what he had to say, even though she didn't agree with it all. Malcolm's bodyguards tried to push her away, but Malcolm restrained them, held her hand, and listened to her patiently. When she had finished, Malcolm said to her, with a gentle empathy that bound Sonia to him forever, "One day you will, sister, one day you will."

And then, Sonia said, "he smiled."

Prince Faysal of Saudi Arabia remembered Malcolm during his 1964 pilgrimage to Mecca: "My first impression of him was, again, an eye-opener for me. Because I saw a different person totally. I didn't see the fiery fire-breather. I saw a very timid, almost shy man. Very quiet, very gentle . . . and it's totally a different picture than what was projected of this man." He continued: "And there were many Americans who came, but none, none, without exception, who had the impact that Malcolm had."

What then, objectively, constitutes the makeup of a hero if it is not selfless dedication to the cause of one's people, the forgoing of a personal or social life, the accomplishment of feats beyond the power of others, and an unforgettable impact upon one's own time?

Malcolm's accomplishments must therefore be seen as a function both of his exceptionality and of the times in which he lived. For all his unmatched talents, for all his wonderful genius, Malcolm might have ended up like so many geniuses before him, a solitary voice crying in the wilderness, if American racism had not intervened to aid him, to make him a prophet in his own country and in every Black person's hometown. Men make history, but only so much history as it is possible for them to make.

MALCOLM AND RACIST RESISTANCE IN AMERICA

Malcolm's slashing critiques of Christianity and the white race for the horrors of slavery won followers throughout the country. Judgment Day is coming, Malcolm said. Allah is going to destroy the immoral white man and restore the Black man, the original Man, to his rightful place. The Nation grew by leaps and bounds.

But it was not just Malcolm's masterful oratory and unstinting work habits that were winning converts to the Nation's point of view. Malcolm had allies in an America that waffled continuously on the explicit promise of racial equality proclaimed by the Supreme Court in 1954. One year later in May, almost to the day, the court issued a follow-up ruling that desegregation must take place "with all deliberate speed." But legal decrees or no, things remained the same for southern Blacks. In Belzoni, Mississippi, two weeks before the court's pronouncement, Reverend George Lee, local leader of the NAACP, was murdered for trying to register to vote.

Then, in August, came the crime that shocked the nation: the murder of fifteen-year-old Emmett Till in Money, Mississippi. Visiting his grandfather for the summer, Till was abducted in the summer night and brutally murdered by two white men for allegedly calling a white woman "Baby" on a dare from his youthful cousins. Showing off his "northern" liberties got young Till slain and thrown into the Tallahatchie River. In September, when word came of the murderers' acquittal, there was hardly a Black person in America who was not outraged.

Despite Mississippi, despite murder, and despite Malcolm, however, most Blacks still believed in the American Way. One such person was Mrs. Rosa Parks, now famous as the woman who sparked the Montgomery bus boycott when she refused to surrender her seat to a white man. After a 381-day struggle by forty thousand Montgomery Blacks, and after several court orders, the Montgomery buses were finally desegregated. Up to that time, that struggle not only was the greatest sustained Black mass movement in southern history; it also brought onto the world stage a new apostle of the philosophy of nonviolence, the Reverend Dr. Martin Luther King, Jr.

In the North, Malcolm scorned both the philosophy and the leader. He went on tirelessly, organizing urban Blacks, increasing Muhammad's flock. Then came the incident of April 1957 that was to bring Malcolm and the Nation of Islam out of the shadows and into the Black spotlight: the savage police beating of Black Muslim Johnson Hinton (Johnson X).

MALCOLM, THE NATION,
BLACK PEOPLE, AND THE POLICE

According to the FBI account taken from the Black newspaper the *Pittsburgh Courier*, a "ruckus" broke out on a Harlem street corner one April evening "when police moved in on a disturbance between a man named Reece V. Poe and an unknown woman." When police began beating Poe, Hinton intervened.

Hinton was a member of Malcolm's Temple No. 7, and a crowd had witnessed his beating. One of their number was a fellow Muslim, who alerted Malcolm and, through their telephone network, other members of the temple's Fruit of Islam. Consequently, when Malcolm arrived at the police station where Hinton had been taken into custody and demanded to see him, more than a hundred Black men and women from the temple were, as Malcolm described it, "standing in rank formation" outside the precinct house.

At first, Malcolm stated, "the police said that he wasn't there. Then they admitted that he was but that I couldn't see him." Noticing the menacing Black people assembled in front of the station, however, the police became "nervous and scared" and turned up a blood-soaked and semiconscious Hinton. Malcolm, angry but firm, demanded that Hinton be given immediate medical attention, so the police called for an ambulance. On foot, Malcolm and the Fruit escorted the ambulance fifteen blocks through Harlem to the hospital, gathering a considerable muttering crowd in their wake. Only when they were assured that their brother was receiving proper care did Malcolm wave his hand, and the Muslims "slipped away." The confrontation and its symbolism quickly became a part of Harlem folklore and is vividly recaptured in Spike Lee's film on Malcolm. More telling, however, was the comment of a white police captain overheard by James Hicks, editor of the *Amsterdam News*: "No man should have that much power." What he really meant, of course, was that it was too much power for any *Black* man to have.

The period of anonymity was over. In his autobiography, Malcolm says:

"For the first time the black man, woman, and child in the streets of Harlem were discussing 'those Muslims.'" Now Malcolm was recognized as a leader in the Harlem community and the Muslims as a legitimate constituency. Hicks asked Malcolm to write a column for the *Amsterdam News*; the *Pittsburgh Courier* requested a column as well; and in Los Angeles, where Malcolm had laid the foundation for Muhammad's Temple No. 27, his articles were featured in the L.A. *Herald-Dispatch*. But it was not just the Black press, the communications lifeline of the national Black community in those days, that had discovered Malcolm. The police now recognized him and the Nation as a great potential danger, because "anyone who can turn off a riot can probably start one."

Police surveillance of Malcolm was stepped up, and in 1958, the FBI, which had opened a file on Malcolm in 1953, designated him a "key figure" (which means that in the event of a race-related situation of national security, Malcolm would be rounded up summarily and held, like the Japanese-Americans of World War II, at the discretion and under the control of the government). He had made the big time.

From this point on, Malcolm would be placed under more intense police and intelligence scrutiny, and the Nation would be subjected to a series of provocative police assaults.

For the moment, however, the police-Muslim conflict would culminate in a Muslim legal victory. Johnson Hinton, suffering from severe brain injuries, had to have a steel plate inserted in his head. With the legal assistance of the Nation, he sued the City of New York and won a seventy-thousand-dollar jury judgment. It was the largest award that had ever been handed down in a case of this kind against the city.

The next encounter between Muslims and the New York police would involve not only members of Temple No. 7 but also a member of Malcolm's own family.

MALCOLM, BETTY, AND THE POLICE

Under Malcolm's custodianship, Temple No. 7 had been attracting scores of young men like Johnson Hinton and those who rushed to his aid that April night in Harlem. The number of women in its ranks had increased as well.

One recent female initiate was a young student from Detroit named Betty Sanders, who attended Booker T. Washington's famed Tuskegee Institute and then came to New York to study nursing. Joining the Nation in 1956 as sister Betty X, she conducted women's classes in health and "medical facts" and somehow came to Malcolm's covert attention. But his idea of courtship was to sit in on her classes from time to time to see "how she was doing."

Curious to find out more about her and get "some idea of her thinking," Malcolm took Betty on an abbreviated visit to the Museum of Natural History. He was impressed by her intelligence and education and surprised to find himself thinking about marriage: "I was so shocked, when I realized *what* I was thinking, I quit going anywhere near Sister Betty X, or anywhere I knew she would be."

But he continued to mull the idea over in his mind, determining "not to say any of that romance stuff that Hollywood and television had filled women's heads with. If I was going to do something, I was going to do it *directly.*"

True to his convictions, Malcolm arranged for Betty to be sent to Chicago so that Mr. Muhammad could check her out. Then he took the plunge.

Driving to Michigan one winter Sunday night to visit his brothers, Malcolm stopped at a gas station early the next morning and—from a pay phone!—called Betty back in New York. He told her that if she wanted to marry him, she should fly out to Detroit right away. Bowled over by the romance of the proposal, she accepted. They were married in his brother Philbert's town of Lansing by "an old hunchbacked white man," before white witnesses.

The two-family house in Queens they moved into, sharing it with another Muslim couple, was violated a few months later by two New York City police detectives and a federal postal inspector. Presenting themselves at the door without a search warrant, the police claimed to be looking for someone neither Malcolm nor Betty had ever heard of. Malcolm demanded that they produce a warrant or leave. The authorities responded by drawing their weapons and firing into the apartment. No one, luckily, was hit. But their neighbor Muslims, hearing the shots, rushed in and began pummeling the officers. Betty, who was pregnant with her first child, and other Muslims were arrested and charged with assaulting a police officer.

Betty's hearing was held the next week. Muslims packed the Queens courthouse. The case did not come to trial until 1959, however, and in the interim, Malcolm and Betty's first child, Attallah, was born.

The trial began in March and lasted ten days. Malcolm attended every day. At its conclusion, he charged: "No black man, even in Mississippi, could have his civil rights violated any worse than what has taken place in Queens County Court House."

Over the next six months, the feud between Malcolm and the New York police intensified. Right after the trial, Malcolm accused the testifying officers of lying, and Betty filed a civil suit against the police. In May, Malcolm disseminated a letter to the press attempting to prove a relationship between the New York police and the Ku Klux Klan. The police commissioner heatedly denied the allegation. In September, Malcolm blasted the police again, this time for being "apathetic" in regard to Black rights.

But these skirmishes in New York paled to insignificance when the next major, one-sided battle broke out in Los Angeles between the Nation and the police.

MALCOLM, MUHAMMAD, AND THE POLICE

The encounter took place in April 1962.

Following a community meeting at the Los Angeles mosque, two Muslims delivering dry cleaning to some members of the mosque were approached by two white police officers, who attempted to search them. An argument began, and several men from the mosque ran to the scene, about a block away, to see about the commotion. In the meantime several squad cars converged, not at the scene of the altercation, but at the mosque.

In the end, mosque secretary Ronald Stokes had been shot, at point blank range, killed by an officer who later testified that he knew Stokes was unarmed, but thought his hands were raised "menacingly." Another Muslim was paralyzed, five others were shot, mostly in the back, and several were beaten. A few officers were also wounded, and one was shot with an officer's pistol, which police later claimed was taken from an officer's holster. No guns were found in the possession of any Muslims.

During the police occupation of the mosque, they lined up all the men against the wall, "deliberately rip[ped] their suit jackets up to the neckline . . . and then rip[ped] each man's trousers from the bottom of the inner seam to the beltloop, before snatching them off." Presumably, the police hoped this humiliation would provoke the Muslims to suicidal retaliation.

It was Johnson Hinton all over again.

Hearing the news, Malcolm told a confederate, "I am going to Los Angeles to die." One reason Malcolm was deeply affected was that he had organized the L.A. mosque himself in 1957. Further, he knew Stokes from Boston, where he had lived only a few blocks from Malcolm's sister Ella, on "the Hill." It is probable that Ronald Stokes, from Roxbury, was originally recruited into the Nation in Boston by Malcolm and was sent out to Los Angeles to play a leadership role in the reorganization of the mosque there.

Enraged by the brazen murder of his old friend, Malcolm flew out to Los Angeles to conduct an investigation and to deliver the eulogy at Stokes's funeral. Two thousand people attended, and a coalition of civil rights groups formed to protest the brutal actions of the police. Foreign leaders like Kwame Nkrumah of Ghana and Gamal Abdel Nasser of Egypt also condemned the murder and the invasion of the mosque.

At a press conference in Los Angeles a few days after the funeral, Malcolm accused the Los Angeles police of shooting down "seven innocent unarmed Black men in cold blood." He asserted that "the Gestapo-type atrocity and the effort to cover up the atrocity with the sanction and support of the American press is in itself a crime against any society that professes to be civilized, religious and God-fearing." That was his public position.

In private, however, Malcolm and many other Muslims awaited instructions from Chicago to avenge their dead.

> They waited on word from the Messenger to begin the Battle of Armageddon that Elijah Muhammad promised would end the era of white supremacy. Instead . . . the message from Chicago . . . instructed them to stick with nonviolence: "Hold fast to Islam. Hold fast to Islam. Allah has promised that no devil will ever get away with the death of a Muslim. We are going out into the streets to begin war with the devil. Not the kind of war he expects . . . No, we are going to let the world know he is the devil: we are going to sell newspapers."

Malcolm chafed but submitted. But many suspected that he was not happy, that he felt the Nation had missed a great opportunity to provide overall leadership to Black people and that it had lost face by not taking action commensurate with its uncompromising rhetoric. It was the first serious clash between Muhammad's organizational conservatism and Malcolm's will to struggle outside the parameters of the Nation.

A week after Malcolm's press conference, an all-white Los Angeles grand jury, with no Muslims testifying, in twenty-three minutes ruled Stokes's death "justifiable homicide." Elijah Muhammad said there was no justice for the Black man in America. The next year—1963—fourteen Muslims involved in the incident were tried on various assault charges, and eleven were convicted.

This was three decades before Rodney King.

THE SCRAMBLE FOR POWER IN THE NATION

In reality, the tensions between Malcolm and the Nation's leadership had been developing for over a year. In 1961, the Messenger's deteriorating bronchial asthmatic condition had forced him to move from Chicago to Phoenix. This meant that Malcolm was now serving two masters and that the Nation had three different leadership centers: the national bureaucracy in Chicago, the Messenger in Phoenix, and Malcolm wherever he happened to be. It was a prescription for trouble, chaos, and intrigue, augmented by the fact that Elijah Muhammad's bad health inevitably raised the question of who would take over the Nation upon his death. To all outsiders and to the press, it was evident who the heir apparent was: the dynamic number-two man, Malcolm X.

But some insiders had other ideas. Ironically, it was Elijah Muhammad himself who had warned Malcolm of this, saying: "Brother Malcolm, I want you to become well known. Because if you are well known, it will make *me* better known . . . but Brother Malcolm, there is something you need to know. You will grow to be hated when you become well known. Because usually people get jealous of public figures." And so it came to pass.

But for a while Malcolm and the Nation were on a roll. After the Johnson Hinton episode in 1957, the Nation's hand had been strengthened by America's continued implacable resistance to racial equality.

In the last week of August, for example, Congress had passed the Civil Rights Bill of 1957, the first federal civil rights law since 1875. Less than a week later, Governor Orval Faubus of Arkansas announced his intention to prevent the integration of Little Rock's Central High School. First, Faubus sent the national guard to bar the nine Black students who sought admission, and then, under federal pressure, he withdrew the guard, leaving the students to the predictable mercy of the fuming racist mob. Faubus's recalcitrance forced President Eisenhower to federalize the guard and deploy more than ten thousand troops to safeguard the Little Rock Nine.

Malcolm said it was all a shell game and that Eisenhower and Faubus were public enemies but private friends. He included more southern stops on his itinerary to hammer home his message of duplicity.

The Nation was booming. Islam was taking root in the prisons; it was in the newspapers and on the radio. Muslim businesses and temples were springing up everywhere. In 1960 Malcolm founded the newspaper that became one of the Nation's most potent vehicles, *Muhammad Speaks*. And Malcolm tried his hand at publishing a magazine, *The Messenger*. Though that effort failed, everything else was working like a charm.

What finally launched Malcolm and the Nation into national and international orbit, bringing them to the awareness of white America and the world, was a five-part television documentary called *The Hate That Hate Produced*, which aired in New York in July 1959. The series came about through the urging of Georgia-born Black writer Louis Lomax, who had approached the TV journalist Mike Wallace to ask if he would be interested in doing something on the Nation of Islam. Wallace had never heard of it but was stunned by what he discovered.

Packaged as an "objective" news program, this summer documentary was actually a call to arms to white America, its Negro supporters and the government to do something to put these "Muslims" back in their place. Wallace's opening statement set the tone of the indictment: ". . . while city officials, state agencies, white liberals and sober-minded Negroes stand idly by, a group of Negro dissenters are taking to street corner stepladders, church pulpits, sports arenas and ballroom platforms across the nation to preach a gospel of hate that would set off a federal investigation if it were to be preached by southern whites. . . ."

The reaction to the show? Malcolm said: "The telephone in our small Temple Seven restaurant nearly jumped off the wall. . . . Calls came long-distance from San Francisco to Maine . . . from even London, Stockholm and Paris . . . it seemed that everywhere I went telephones were ringing." And contrary to Mike Wallace's hopes, membership in the Nation doubled.

Like Christopher Columbus "discovering" the "New World" that had always been there, America now discovered Malcolm and the Nation.

When the series aired, Malcolm was on his first trip out of the country, visiting newly independent Ghana and several states in the Middle East as an emissary for Mr. Muhammad. Upon his return, the firestorm of coverage that would follow Malcolm for the rest of his life was blazing. All the national magazines wanted stories, and a Black writer named Alex Haley would soon publish a piece on the Nation for *Reader's Digest*. And in 1961 Dr. C. Eric Lincoln's revealing study, *The Black Muslims in America*, was published. Malcolm began to receive invitations to speak on white college campuses. (In a few years, he would be the second-most-popular speaker on the college circuit, after Barry Goldwater.)

In 1960, Malcolm and the southern freedom movement seemed to explode together. In Greensboro, students at North Carolina A & T triggered the sit-in movement that would in turn lead to the formation of the Student Nonviolent Coordinating Committee (SNCC), whose members historian Howard Zinn called the New Abolitionists. Young people on college campuses and in the movement would become an important part of Malcolm's unofficial constituency. Oblivious of Marcus Garvey and W. E. B. Du Bois, the students would be more open to

Malcolm's critique than to the views of the older, more traditional, "sober-minded Negroes" Mike Wallace favored.

While America's television screens were filled nightly with scenes from the Battle to Desegregate the South, ten African nations became independent and took their seats in the United Nations. Malcolm, too, expanded his international ties. He met with Mr. Wachuku, Speaker of the Nigerian House, and with Fidel Castro. In fact, it is rumored that Malcolm helped to facilitate Castro's move to the Hotel Theresa in Harlem when downtown hotels hassled the Cubans. And in October, Malcolm helped sponsor a huge Harlem rally to welcome Kwame Nkrumah, the new president of Ghana. Despite Mr. Muhammad's warning, Malcolm was permitting himself to become quite the public figure.

MALCOLM, MUHAMMAD, AND KENNEDY

The "Negro question" had become the dominant theme in domestic American life, and the Black vote promised to be pivotal in this election year of 1960. Democratic candidate John F. Kennedy shrewdly bid for the vote by intervening to aid Martin Luther King, jailed in Georgia for participating in an Atlanta sit-in. Kennedy telephoned Mrs. Coretta King and had his brother Robert call the Georgia authorities to ensure that nothing untoward happened to Dr. King while in their custody. King's father, "Daddy" King, a lifelong Republican, announced that he had seen the light and endorsed JFK. Kennedy got the overwhelming Black vote, and won a narrow victory over Richard Nixon.

Blacks took this demonstrated concern for Dr. King to be an indication of Kennedy's support for their struggle, the second great promise after *Brown*. They, too, hoped to be part of Camelot.

Then came 1961. Muhammad, from his retreat in Phoenix, gave Malcolm free rein as national representative for the Nation. This near-coronation was seen as an ominous development by those who feared what would happen to them if Malcolm took over. They were already upset about the way Malcolm seemed to be putting "his" people in key spots around the country. Louis X, head of the Boston mosque, was thought to be in "Malcolm's camp," and it was believed Malcolm had installed men loyal to him in mosques around the country. In addition, Malcolm's brother Philbert was minister of Lansing's mosque and Wilfred, minister of Temple No. 1 in Detroit.

There was something else, as tricky as the human interplay between gratitude and resentment, in members of Mr. Muhammad's family whom Malcolm had befriended. Malcolm had thought it a shame that Muhammad's children "worked as some of them did for the white man . . . I felt that I should work for Mr. Muhammad's family as sincerely as I worked for him. I urged Mr. Muhammad to let me put on a special drive . . . to raise funds which would enable those of his children working for the white man to be instead employed within the Nation."

What, then, was the reaction of family members who owed their new station in life to an outsider who now threatened to take their father's place? We know that some of Muhammad's family had great affection for Malcolm. But how widespread was that attitude? And did Malcolm feel that the family owed him something, that they should be indebted to him in some way? Resentment, gratitude, charity, and patronage constitute an awkward and volatile human mix. We can only wonder what part these feelings played in the drama about to unfold.

There was another consideration: By Muhammad's own admission, Malcolm was "the best money-raiser" in the Nation. And no one wants to kill the goose that lays the golden egg. Malcolm's very success had made him vulnerable, however. In building an economically viable national organization, he had now created one strong enough to go on without him. The money was in the coffers. The challenge for Malcolm's adversaries was to keep it there, and also keep Malcolm from taking over the Nation.

The Nation subsisted, in large measure, on tithing its members. It was the members who raised the money to make Muhammad's family independent of white largesse. It was the members who had financed Muhammad's trip to Mecca, and it was the members who purchased Muhammad's house in Phoenix. The membership was the financial lifeblood of the organization. Photographer Gordon Parks, covering the Nation of Islam for *Life*, observed that Muslims pay staggering dues of $8 weekly, plus extra assessments. We have noted some of those extra assessments above. But if that observation is accurate, it meant that the Nation's income, which, when Malcolm joined was around $160,000 a year, had ballooned in 1960 (even if we take the lowest estimate of thirty thousand members) to $12 million yearly. If the thirty thousand members doubled after the broadcast of *The Hate That Hate Produced*, that would mean $24 million. Some scholars estimated that Muslim membership in its heyday ran as high as 100,000. Whatever the actual number was, the problem facing anyone who wished to get rid of Malcolm was how to do it so as to neither alienate the membership nor permit Malcolm to carry the membership away with him. That dilemma was compounded by another problem: how to separate Malcolm from Elijah Muhammad. Because so long as Malcolm had Elijah Muhammad's support, no one could move against Malcolm openly.

Then human weakness, as it nearly always does, provided the answer.

ADULTERY, ASSASSINATION, AND ANNULMENT

"Around 1963, if anyone had noticed, I spoke less and less of religion. I taught social doctrine to Muslims, and current events, and politics. I stayed wholly off the subject of morality. And the reason for this was that . . . I had discovered Muslims had been betrayed by Elijah Muhammad himself."

Malcolm X

For years, there had been hints of sexual impropriety in Chicago. They were substantiated in late 1962, when, Malcolm writes, he "learned reliably that numerous Muslims were leaving Mosque Two" because several of Muhammad's secretaries were said to have borne him children. . . . Adultery! "Why, any Muslim guilty of adultery was summarily ousted in disgrace." Malcolm had been confronted with the reality of the rumors when he came upon two of the secretaries outside Muhammad's home during one of his monthly visits there.

Deeply agitated, Malcolm went to Chicago to see Mr. Muhammad's son Wallace, the family member who Malcolm felt was most "objective" and with whom he "shared an exceptional closeness and trust."

Wallace, according to Malcolm, confirmed the rumors, prompting Malcolm to break the rule "that no Muslim is supposed to have any contact with another Muslim in the 'isolated state'" (suspension from the company of other Muslims) and went to see three of Mr. Muhammad's former secretaries. They told him that, indeed, Muhammad had fathered their children. "I felt almost out of my mind," revealed Malcolm.

After pondering what to do next, Malcolm wrote to Muhammad about "the poison being spread against him" and then flew to Phoenix in April 1963. Before going, however, Malcolm and Wallace researched the Scriptures and the Koran for religious precedents and rationales. They decided that the best tactic would be to explain Muhammad's indiscretions as "the fulfillment of prophecy." This was the defense Malcolm proposed, and Muhammad concurred. "I'm David," he said. "When you read about how David took another man's wife, I'm that David. You read about Noah, who got drunk—that's me. You read about Lot, who went and laid up with his own daughters. I have to fulfill all those things."

Then Malcolm made a strategic error from which he would find it impossible to recover. He told six East Coast Muslim ministers, so that they would not "be caught by surprise and shock" if they had to teach the "prophecy" defense. Malcolm discovered that some of them had already heard about the out-of-wedlock children. What he didn't anticipate was that "the Chicago Muslim officials" and other ministers would accuse Malcolm of "throwing gasoline on the fire instead of water."

Malcolm had given his enemies the wedge. They set out to pry him irrevocably away from Elijah Muhammad.

In fact, the first salvos in the battle to undermine Malcolm had already been fired. In 1962, Malcolm noticed that *Muhammad Speaks*, the newspaper he had founded, was saying less and less about him. "Mr. Muhammad's son, Herbert, now the paper's publisher, had instructed that as little as possible be printed about me . . . finally I got no coverage at all—for by now an order had been given to completely black me out of the newspaper."

The campaign Chicago now launched against Malcolm was the latest development in the tug-of-war that had been going on since Muhammad had moved to Phoenix. Malcolm, for example, would speak before thousands, only to be ignored by Chicago. In Malcolm's view, Chicago was trying to cut him down to size, discouraging him from holding large rallies (and thus getting him off the front pages). Malcolm ignored them and staged even larger rallies. The Chicago contingent seems at one point to have been successful in getting its point of view across to Muhammad, who evidently told Malcolm to stop speaking at white colleges because such appearances did not gain the Nation converts and provided opportunities to be "blasted" by the press. Malcolm replied that he would accede to Muhammad's wishes, but he'd need to fulfill those engagements he had already agreed to. This response illuminates the tension between Malcolm's sense of personal duty and Nation policies. It was an omen of things to come.

At any rate, although Malcolm did not stop appearing on white campuses, somehow the issue was resolved. The next clash of views occurred in reaction to the murder of Stokes, the invasion of the mosque in Los Angeles, and Elijah Muhammad's directive to sell newspapers as an act of retribution. Indeed, the newspaper question took on an even stranger dimension when Raymond Sharrieff, son-in-law of Elijah Muhammad and national captain of the Fruit of Islam, sent out a letter informing every Muslim that he must obtain at least two subscriptions to *Muhammad Speaks* daily or be expelled from the mosque. And this at the very time when Black Los Angeles still smoldered from the Stokes slaying. The difference in priorities between Chicago and Malcolm could hardly have been rendered more starkly.

Outside of internal politics, things were going pretty well for the Nation. The State of New York had decreed that Muslims had the right to practice their religion in prison; Malcolm was critiquing Dr. King's new nonviolent movement in Albany, Georgia, with his usual devastating and deprecating wit; and his status in Harlem was assured among the street folk and broadening among the mainstream leadership. Malcolm debated representatives from CORE—the Congress of Racial Equality—and the NAACP and spoke at Adam Clayton Powell Jr.'s Abyssinian Baptist Church. He began his autobiography with Alex Haley. He tried again to repair his damaged relationship with Muhammad by writing a letter of explanation and apology. He told Muhammad that they should work together and not let themselves be divided. However, that very letter had the smell of equal status about it rather than the total submission of old. Malcolm's sense of his own importance in his own right was becoming palpable.

Muhammad was too ill to preside over Savior's Day that year, so Malcolm ran the convention, even dictating the roles of Muhammad's family. He then stayed in Chicago, speaking and giving interviews, for weeks after the convention was over. Resenting his role at the convention, his usurpation of their turf, and his attempts to advise them, Muhammad's family members appealed to Muhammad to get Malcolm out of Chicago.

The rupture was fast becoming inevitable. Malcolm was speaking out more and more on political matters. He blasted Martin Luther King's leadership of the demonstrations in Birmingham, and he blasted President Kennedy's refusal to send troops to protect the civil rights demonstrators, saying he didn't have the legal power to do so. But "without any new law being written," Kennedy did send in federal troops to quell the May 1963 Black rebellion in Birmingham, after the home of King's brother, A. D., was bombed, along with the Gaston Motel, where Martin himself had been staying. The Black masses of Birmingham saw these twin bombings as an attempt by the Klan to torpedo the agreement King had made with the Birmingham city fathers and an attempt to assassinate King himself. They went out into the streets in the very first of the urban rebellions that would convulse the land for the next half decade. (In 1961, sneering at "nonviolence," Malcolm predicted an uprising in the Black South. Now he could say: I told you so.)

But the reactionary elements of the white South were not deterred from their policy of terrorist resistance. In June, Medgar Evers, state secretary of the NAACP in Mississippi, was shot to death on his front steps. Muhammad instructed Malcolm "not to assist the NAACP or any other organization in civil rights demonstrations." In August, the March on Washington was held, and Malcolm derided it as "the Farce in Washington." Again Muhammad ordered all Muslims not to participate. Malcolm didn't participate, but he went to Washington to express himself on the march, which he viewed as co-opted. Less than three weeks after the march, the Sixteenth Street Baptist Church, a headquarters of the recently concluded Birmingham Movement, was bombed, and four Black girls were killed.

The pace of events was causing Malcolm to feel more and more frustrated. "When a high-powered rifle slug tore through the back of the NAACP Field Secretary Medgar Evers in Mississippi, *I wanted to say the blunt truths that needed to be said.* When a bomb was exploded in a Negro Christian church in Birmingham, Alabama, snuffing out the lives of those four beautiful little black girls, I made comments—*but not what should have been said* about the climate of hate that the American white man was generating." (Emphasis mine.) Soon would come Malcolm's opportunity to say "the blunt truths that needed to be said." On November 22, 1963, shortly before Thanksgiving, John Fitzgerald Kennedy, thirty-fifth president of the United States, was assassinated in Dallas. Muhammad ordered all Muslims to refrain from comment. But on December 1, in New York City, Malcolm substituted for Muhammad, speaking on "God's Judgment of White America."

During the question-and-answer period, Malcolm was asked about Kennedy's assassination. Elijah Muhammad had sent out *two* directives instructing his ministers to say "No comment." Malcolm, however, set the context for his response to the assassination by naming the many leaders in Africa, Latin America, and Southeast Asia who had been killed as a result of American intervention, and ended by saying that he "honestly felt that it was . . . a case of chickens coming home to roost."

That week, Malcolm made his regular visit to Muhammad and was told that he was to be silenced for ninety days to dissociate the rest of the Muslims from his "bad statement."

He was forbidden to talk with the press or even to teach in his own mosque. Later, a qualification was added by Chicago: Malcolm would be reinstated in ninety days "if he submits."

The Nation's official statement sounded more like a court-martial than a temporary rebuke. The situation put Malcolm in a quandary because he loved the Nation and he loved Elijah Muhammad, but he did not agree with the Nation's obdurate refusal to involve itself in the Black struggle exploding all around the country.

Malcolm knew many movement people, and even where he disagreed with them, he respected what most were trying to do. He had, in fact, become a de facto link between the Nation and the movement: He had assisted Percy Sutton in voter registration, he had spoken out against police brutality, and he had joined the 28th Precinct Community Council, which officially extended Harlem's greetings to African dignitaries at the United Nations. Malcolm had even adopted some of the tactics of the civil rights movement, leading the Fruit of Islam in a protest demonstration in Times Square after the New York police had harassed Muslims trying to sell *Muhammad Speaks* on 42nd Street. Clearly, in the best of all possible worlds, what Malcolm wanted was to unite the Nation with the movement—and frighten America to death.

But the conservative element in the Nation's leadership did not share Malcolm's dream; and Elijah Muhammad—in faraway Phoenix, in bad health, physically unable to travel to see and experience what Malcolm was seeing and experiencing and relating to—did not seem to share it either.

Malcolm and the Nation had reached an impasse. Torn between relevance and refuge, torn between speaking out and lying low, torn between the front line and the sidelines, Malcolm could no more resist injecting himself into the high-stakes game of American Racial Poker than he could stop breathing. He "raised" America's cards by telling it that its "chickens had come home to roost." But Elijah Muhammad called his hand.

In Their Own Words

Osman Ahmed	Friend; Dartmouth student
Maya Angelou	Writer
Peter Bailey	Student; Harlem civil rights activist
John Henrik Clarke	Historian; associate of Malcolm X
Ossie Davis	Actor; activist
William DeFossett	New York police officer
Muriel Feelings	Student
Peter Goldman	Journalist
Alex Haley	Coauthor of *The Autobiography of Malcolm X*
Benjamin Karim	Assistant minister, Mosque No. 7; close associate of Malcolm X
John Lewis	Member of SNCC
Wilfred Little	Malcolm X's eldest brother
Stanley Malone	One of the lawyers representing Muslims in Los Angeles mosque incident
Robert Mangum	Deputy commissioner, N.Y.P.D., a negotiator, along with Malcolm X, in the Johnson Hinton police brutality incident in Harlem
Imam Wallace D. Mohammed	Formerly known as Wallace D. Muhammad, son of Elijah Muhammad
Abdul Aziz Omar	Formerly Philbert Little, Malcolm X's elder brother
Gordon Parks	*Life* photographer
Amina Rahman	Formerly Sharon X, civil rights activist who joined Nation of Islam as a teenager; close associate of Malcolm X
Gloria Richardson	Civil rights leader in Cambridge, Maryland; associate of Malcolm X
Attallah Shabazz	Malcolm X's eldest daughter
Betty Shabazz	Wife of Malcolm X
Yusuf Shah	Formerly Captain Joseph, Fruit of Islam, Mosque No. 7
Alice Windom	Friend and associate of Malcolm X in Africa

When I first heard about Malcolm, I thought he was a pigment of somebody else's imagination. He sounded so mean and so tough and so cruel. I thought the white people, they made him up.

Maya Angelou

Muslim rally, with Fruit of Islam member standing guard before podium, 1961.

Malcolm always wanted to go to New York. That was his ultimate plan. He used to say that he would rather be an assistant minister in New York than be a minister anywhere else in the country.

But he knew he couldn't just walk in there. So he went to Boston, he went to Philadelphia, and he did good there. Mr. Muhammad began to have some problems with the wife of the minister in New York. That's how Malcolm got to New York. Mr. Muhammad, who was absolute boss, sent him there.

Yusuf Shah

125th Street and Eighth Avenue,
Harlem, ca. 1956.

As soon as Malcolm got into New York, it began to expand—right out of the little old storefront there. Malcolm used to go out on the street in Harlem and start teaching. And have hundreds and hundreds of people listen to what he said and accept Islam.

Abdul Aziz Omar

A Hundred and Twenty-fifth Street was, as we said, the Black capital of the world. Is it Trafalgar Square, London, where you have the public speakers? Well, that was *our* public forum area. You had several corners assigned to certain people. On the southwest corner, for instance, a fella by the name of Carlos Cooks, he had some kind of African movement going. All those corners were staked out.

William DeFossett

Elijah Muhammad
and his son, Wallace
D. Muhammad, in
front of a portrait
of W. Fard
Muhammad,
founder of
the Nation
of Islam.

Had Elijah Muhammad tried to introduce an orthodox form of Arab-oriented Islam, I doubt if he would have attracted five hundred people. But he introduced a form of Islam that could communicate with the people he had to deal with. And he didn't steal them from the little church, big church, or the lodges, he found a haven for the people who had no haven. He was the king to those who had no king, and he was the messiah to those who some people thought unworthy of a messiah.

John Henrik Clarke

Street speaker, 125th Street, 1938–39, a Harlem tradition.

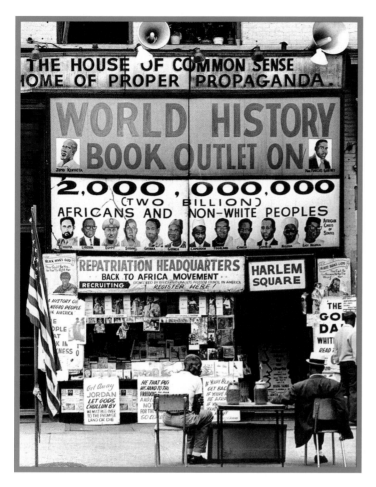

National Memorial
African Bookstore,
Harlem, 1964.

Malcolm established his base in front of Elder Michaux's National Memorial African Bookstore. They used to have big rallies out there periodically. The thing that would attract you right away with Malcolm and his group was the appearance and the discipline. They were the best-looking group you could find out there on the street.

William DeFossett

In those early days the main thing they were after was just gettin' rid of that inferiority complex that existed among our people and spreading this new idea. That's what Malcolm began to do.

Wilfred Little

He was saying some pretty rough things, particularly about whites. And those of us who wanted to keep peace with the white world—some of us, you know, had our jobs out in the white community—we didn't really want to get too close to Malcolm.

Ossie Davis

Facing Page: Muslim convention, Uline
Arena, Washington, D.C., 1961.

University of Islam, Chicago, 1963.

Woman shouts epithets at Elizabeth Eckford, one of the nine Black students who desegregated Central High School, Little Rock, Arkansas, September 4, 1957.

Muslim convention, Uline
Arena, Washington, D.C., 1961.
In foreground on walkie-talkie
is Elijah Muhammad, Jr.

There was a gulf between the Nation of Islam, our philosophy and our liturgy, and the civil rights movement. Number one, we didn't allow whites into our meetings. Two, we did not propagate integration. We believed that we needed schools that taught our own history. We believed that America was going to be destroyed because of her history and what had happened to us here. We didn't see a future here in this country.

Benjamin Karim

We were very militant, you know? We saluted, we drilled, we marched with cut corners. That attracts women and men. We used to dress alike. Sometimes we'd wear blue suits, sometimes gray, sometimes brown. Because that showed unity. And that's what we did. That attracted people.

Yusuf Shah

The 28th Precinct was notorious for their prejudice. Most of the personnel were Caucasians. They had a few Blacks, but they weren't what you'd call commanding positions— no captains or anything. Naturally, when the people saw us come out there, that was the first time anyone had marched on the 28th Precinct in protest.

Yusuf Shah

At the time I was a deputy commissioner downtown. I received a call from the 28th Precinct that there was a demonstration of Muslims in front of the police station and that Malcolm X was in the station. A police officer had assaulted one of his members, they said, and Malcolm was demanding a full investigation. He said he would only talk to the *Amsterdam News* editor, Jimmy Hicks, and to Bob Mangum. He wanted my word that I would see to it that an investigation of the assault was held in the police department. He wanted Jimmy's word that he would publicize it in the newspaper.

Robert Mangum

The atmosphere was, I think the word they use is *charged*. Well, this atmosphere was explosive.

William DeFossett

From the corner of Seventh Avenue to the corner of Eighth, which is a very long block, they had Black males all dressed in black, immaculate. Standing at parade rest and interspersed with them were females dressed completely in white. And they were making no sound. Covering the whole length of the block. Across the street from the precinct.

Robert Mangum

It was eerie to see at two or three o'clock in the morning. You just heard feet shuffling. Hundreds and hundreds of feet. Just shuffling around and around.

William DeFossett

When the people heard the sirens and seen us walking around, they became curious. There was about three, four thousand people out there in a matter of seconds. The policemen, they was just upset, they had never seen anything like this before. 'Cause it was spontaneous. This is what made the 28th Precinct acquiesce to our demands that Johnson Hinton be taken to the hospital.

Yusuf Shah

This brain surgeon, Dr. Thomas Matthews, performed a very delicate operation, and he saved Johnson's life.

A sergeant tried to make the Muslims leave, but Malcolm said, they won't move for you. He said, I'll send them away. He went out to the front of the station, on the first step, and just waved his hand.

Robert Mangum

There'd been police brutality in Harlem before, long before. But when the Nation of Islam put a solid force in front of the hospital, and another in front of the police precinct, the police said that no one man should have that much power. It frightened the police, because they didn't believe anybody in Harlem was that organized. I believe it was at this time and after, with some consistency, that they began to plan the death of Malcolm X.

John Henrik Clarke

Muslims picketing a police station, Harlem, late 1950s.

Malcolm knew that there were ministers that were a little envious of him. He had an old Chevrolet before he got this Oldsmobile. And Mr. Muhammad had told him to buy himself a new car, because Malcolm drove like a race-car driver down the highway, and traveling to different places, the car could break down, and he would be stranded. The reason he wouldn't go and buy a car was, he said, because he didn't want the other ministers to become jealous of him. Finally Captain Joseph and Secretary Maceo went and bought the car for him.

Benjamin Karim

Top: Malcolm X gets into Oldsmobile, in front of building housing Temple No. 7, Lenox Avenue and 116th Street, Harlem, 1963.
Bottom: Banner on side of bus advertising Nation of Islam event, 1961.

Mr. Muhammad made an appearance in Washington, D.C., at the Uline Arena in 1959. We had 10,000 people. Louis Lomax asked Malcolm could he get Mr. Muhammad to sit for an interview with him, not with Mike Wallace. Mr. Muhammad told Malcolm no. It wasn't gonna do any good, all it would do is hurt us in our work. Malcolm wasn't satisfied; he continued to ask, and Mr. Muhammad reluctantly agreed. So Mike Wallace puts his film together, *The Hate That Hate Produced*. They did exactly what Mr. Muhammad said. Malcolm was embarrassed, because he had assured Mr. Muhammad that they wouldn't do it. Mr. Muhammad had to show Malcolm that these people do nothing but deal in tricks.

Yusuf Shah

George Lincoln Rockwell and other members of the American Nazi Party at Nation of Islam convention, Uline Arena, Washington, D.C., 1961.

Captain Joseph at podium, Fruit of Islam night, Harlem, early 1960s.

Harlem is the capital of Black America, New York is the media capital of America. I think Malcolm, with the gift he had for understanding the media and the uses of the media, understood that and wanted to be where the action was, wanted to be at the center.

Peter Goldman

In his house, Malcolm X had a room set aside for the production of the first paper for the Nation of Islam, *Muhammad Speaks*. He would have pages plastered all over the wall and notes, sheets of paper he was making notes on. Those were all over the wall, too. The whole room was just turned into a workplace for the production of the paper. And he had a typewriter and was typing with two fingers. But he typed very fast, very fast.

Imam Wallace D. Mohammed

The white media's portrayal of Brother Malcolm had one major goal, which was to turn the Black community away from him, if possible; to make sure that he did not get too many supporters and followers. The Black media, on the other hand, had members who were very negative toward him, but they always qualified it, because of his appeal in the larger Black community.

Peter Bailey

Malcolm X and
Premier Fidel Castro
of Cuba at the Hotel
Theresa, Harlem,
September 19, 1960.

Demonstration at the Hotel
Theresa, Harlem, fall 1960.

The symbols were absolutely magnificent. Fidel Castro in a Black-owned hotel, Khrushchev meeting him in the lobby, the community surrounding the hotel day and night. Castro occasionally coming to the window to wave. It was an event in the development of consciousness in the community.

John Henrik Clarke

From '57 on, we saw this burgeoning of independence of Africans resuming the ability to govern themselves after years of colonialism. Suddenly those of us in the States who had grown up on Tarzan movies and all the degradation of African people were seeing these marvelous people coming into the United Nations—the men being so dignified, the women looking gorgeous in their traditional attire—hearing speeches being made in perfect English that were striking home at what needed to be done for Africa to resume its rightful place in the world. And we realized that we had been lied to.

Alice Windom

President Kwame Nkrumah addresses a rally in front of the Hotel Theresa, Harlem, October 5, 1960. Malcolm X is at lower right.

A Nation of Islam bazaar, New York, early
1960s. Betty Shabazz is in front row.

Uline Arena, Washington, D.C., 1961.

Men at rally featuring Malcolm X, Harlem,
March 23, 1963.

We were growing in leaps and bounds, thousands and thousands of people. Money had increased ten thousand percent, and there had to be someone there that knew how to organize it. Most of these people came from Malcolm, through Chicago as the headquarters. The Honorable Elijah Muhammad, he got less and less busy.

Abdul Aziz Omar

The Harlem of Malcolm's time is not the Harlem a young person sees today. The streets were clean in the sixties. The air would be crackling with excitement. The African Americans who call themselves Ethiopians would be out. The Black Jews would be out. The Nation of Islam, Baptists, Methodists, Holy Rollers, Seventh Day Adventists, all the religious groups would be out, and the two Black atheists in the world would be there. Somebody with a conga drum or with bongo drums would be *pa pa ta ka ta ta ka pa ta ka*. There would be aromas. People selling tamales in pushcarts and hot dogs and barbecue. Aromas and sounds, and the air would pop like chewing gum.

Maya Angelou

Outdoor rally, June 1963.

All Nation of Islam ministers were schooled, particularly those most able, to be oratorical acrobats. It was almost oratorical calisthenics, while maintaining an image of great cool. Malcolm was simply the most dramatic of all that I ever saw. And he trained others. And all of them were trained by Mr. Elijah Muhammad.

Alex Haley

I saw Malcolm for the very first time in person on the corner of a Hundred and Twenty-fifth Street and Seventh Avenue, telling off about four hundred white cops with guns on their hips what he thought about them. I thought, *how long is this young man gonna live like that.*

Gordon Parks

Outdoor rally,
June 1963.

I've seen Malcolm make men cry, and strong women. Seen him bring a crowd to the point of wanting to riot and pull them back from the edge very quickly. He could almost play them, move them back and forth, dancing close to the edge, but with just incredible control.

Amina Rahman

When Malcolm would ascend the little platform, he couldn't talk for the first four or five minutes, the people would be making such a praise-shout to him.

Maya Angelou

Outdoor rally in front of Hotel
Theresa, Harlem, 1963.

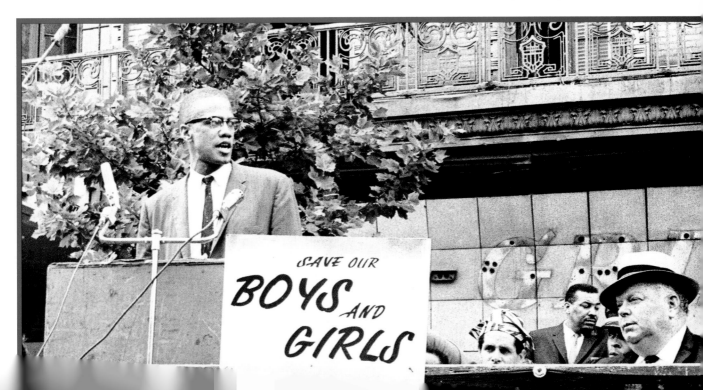

Benjamin Karim stands behind Malcolm X with an umbrella, Harlem, June 29, 1963.

Street crowd listening to Malcolm X, Harlem, June 1963.

Malcolm X with Fruit of Islam guards and assistant ministers, 115th Street and Lenox Avenue, Harlem, 1963.

I was holding an umbrella over his head. It started drizzling. Now, I'm looking at this crowd while the Minister's talking. People stopped blinking their eyelids, as though they were in a trance. Then you would see somebody—probably the fluid evaporated on the eyeball, and they realized something was amiss—as though they had come out of a trance. Then they'd go right back into it, without blinking. It was strange. It started raining, but all of those people stayed, thousands, blocking off the street for two blocks in both directions.

Benjamin Karim

People use that cliché, "the university of the streets." But that really was the university of the street, because it was a tremendous learning experience. And it was the beginning of why I generally call Malcolm a master teacher. More than anything else, that's what he was.

Peter Bailey

I was resistant to the Nation because I had antipathy toward any one single figure being anybody's savior. The kind of adulation that comes out of that kind of church setting means it eventually corrupts that person, and it is open for fascist tendencies. They had this regimented kind of life, and they could only do what Elijah Muhammad told them. I distrusted that.

Gloria Richardson

Once you heard him speak, you never went back to where you were before. Even if you kept your position, you had to rethink it. For me, it was literally an awakening. I would go down every Saturday to listen, and if he mentioned a magazine article or a book, we would rush right out to the library to get it.

Peter Bailey

It was not just his person, it was his message. It was his ability to arrange it in his own way—it was nothing new, you know. Just like with a piece of cloth, it is your ability as a designer to make different designs from this same piece of cloth. That's what he could do. He could make a different design out of history than what's normally written in the books.

Benjamin Karim

A Muslim temple meeting, Harlem, ca. 1962. Malcolm X is at podium.

Malcolm X with Muslim children at the Museum of Natural History, New York, 1963.

Fruit of Islam members, Chicago, 1963.

I liked the male role of taking an assertive attitude in terms of his family, and the protection. I know a lot of women who were drawn to the movement because of some of the philosophy, more than the religion. I was more taken with the philosophy of self-determination.

Muriel Feelings

I joined the Nation in part because it was so radically different from everything else around me at the time, and because I admired, and more important, trusted Malcolm. I was still in high school. There were things I didn't understand, and I didn't believe in some of the philosophy and rhetoric of the Nation of Islam at that time. But Malcolm was there, and Malcolm was a leader.

Amina Rahman

We did calisthenics. We did karate. We'd do judo—all the kinda stuff that builds the individual up. And how not to eat pork and how to cook our food done. And how to treat our wives properly. In the meantime, sisters were put into women's classes. They taught 'em how to sew, cook, how to treat their husbands, raise their children, and in general how to act at home and abroad. Naturally, the brothers and the sisters begin to shine like new money.

Abdul Aziz Omar

Above: Harlem, ca. 1961. *Below*: Muslim men standing at attention, Chicago, 1963.

Malcolm was a student of etymology. He loved words. He said words have histories, like people. And he used to break down this word *Negro*. He showed it means we are people who are mentally and spiritually dead. The word *Negro* simply means you're a dead man, from your neck up.

Benjamin Karim

The X meant you no longer was a drinker, a smoker, you no longer practiced adultery and fornication—so you were *ex* all those things that were negative. You were *ex* no more of those things that kept you down, and now you qualified to strengthen yourself as a servant of God. So we became X.

Abdul Aziz Omar

Malcolm related to us through himself, through his struggle. One example was, the Minister made such an impact on Brother Gladstone that he just stopped cold turkey from using drugs. One day Gladstone told us that a police detective, who heard Gladstone was now coming to the temple, had left some drugs for him at a candy store on Lenox Avenue. Gladstone went over there, and sure enough, heroin had been left. The detective couldn't believe that Gladstone could have heard anything powerful and persuasive enough to cause him to quit using drugs.

Benjamin Karim

We didn't go to movies anymore. We rented movies and we would bring them to the mosque to show. We didn't have parties as we did in our "dead lives," as we used to say. We did not have girlfriends. You were required to marry or to leave a woman alone. We had some very strict codes of ethics. You can understand that we would have to have somewhere we could gather, as birds of a feather gathering together.

Benjamin Karim

Temple No. 7 Restaurant, Harlem,
early 1960s.

Our social life was geared around the mosque and the restaurant. It served, as they say in Arabic, *halal*, or the Jews say kosher, food. If Minister Malcolm was in town, he was there, and we would sit around the table and drink coffee and eat bean pie and ice cream. And there was a sister, Lana, who was one of the greatest cooks that God ever allowed to have a spoon in her hand.

Benjamin Karim

When Elijah Muhammad came from Chicago to visit the 369th Armory, the Fruit of Islam established a security procedure. The armory must have had close to ten thousand people. And everyone that came in was searched. Male and female. Very efficiently and very quickly. If you had a nail file, they took it off you. When you came back out, you got your nail file. That armory, that afternoon, was one of the safest places in the world.

William DeFossett

The Fruit of Islam, these were the absolute baddest, cleanest brothers I'd ever seen in my life. Nobody was going to be snatching no pocket books from no Muslim sister in Harlem. They knew that if they did, they would be in trouble.

Peter Bailey

Elijah Muhammad and Malcolm X at the
369th Armory, Harlem, 1960.

Muslim self-defense instruction, Chicago, 1963.

I was surprised to see them training German shepherd dogs for attack dogs. They had their arms bandaged so when the dog attacked, they wouldn't be injured. It was amazing to watch that. And Malcolm would look at me and smile. And he said, if the brothers can face that dog with its vicious fangs, they can face a lot of other things.

Gordon Parks

Muslim man with notebook open to Nation of Islam teachings about the role of men, Chicago, 1963.

Malcolm X and Redd Foxx (*right*), Temple No. 7
Restaurant, Harlem, early 1960s.

You might walk into the restaurant and Redd Foxx is standing there talking to Minister Malcolm, because they knew each other before he became a Muslim and before he went to prison. Gordon Parks, I think he was the first person that Minister Malcolm allowed to come into the mosque and take pictures, or to film. So the restaurant was also a learning place.

Benjamin Karim

I worked after school in the *Muhammad Speaks* newspaper office, which doubled as the temple office and Malcolm's office. One Saturday morning I arrived and wanted the typewriter moved to my desk. Well, Malcolm and several brothers were there talking. So I picked up the typewriter and moved it to the desk.

Malcolm turns to me and says, "Sister, you just insulted every brother in this room." I said, "What did I do?" "You moved that typewriter instead of calling on a brother for help and allowing the brother to be a man, and, you know, taking your place as a woman who needs to rely on men to do things like that." Later on I said I didn't understand his choice in attacking me instead of a brother. He said that would have heaped more criticism and scorn on this Black man. This way, he would be making the point to them and to me just as effectively without making them feel even worse.

Amina Rahman

Malcolm and Betty at home in East Elmhurst, Queens, with Attallah and Qubilah, ca. 1961.

My mother set the rhythm in our household, and, at least from the perspective of the child, my father was certainly a supporter and a contributor to what the energies were in my household. But since it was my mother who was the housewife and round-the-clock role model for me, my mother was my first love. My father was my first buddy.

Attallah Shabazz

Malcolm with Qubilah and Attallah, 1962.

"A Night with the Fruit of Islam" dinner, New York, early 1963. Malcolm X and wife Betty at main table with special guests from the Harlem community, southern Africa, and other mosques.

He was a prolific reader. He could deal with a difficult book in three or four hours. He was just very observant and very analytical. And he says, "Girl, when I was in prison, there was so much time that if a fly flew through a window, you would not say, 'the fly flew through the window,' you would say, 'the fly flew through the lower right-hand quadrant and landed on its front legs.'"

Betty Shabazz

In Malcolm X's shadow cabinet there were different people who had expertise on different subjects. I was the man in history and historical information and personalities. There were other people on politics, another person occasionally on sociology. The diversity of people in this shadow cabinet, none of them Muslims, was equivalent to the faculty of a good university.

John Henrik Clarke

Muhammad Speaks was a kind of international paper for us Africans, because it was the only paper which used to bring in fullness what was going on on the African continent. A lot of African students used to read it, used to listen to Brother Malcolm, because the aspirations of the Africans in the 1960s were really voiced and aired by Malcolm.

Osman Ahmed

The Nation of Islam during the early sixties, 1962, was perhaps enjoying its best days in terms of enthusiasm. We were realizing a sense of achievement—opening restaurants, grocery stores, seeing *Muhammad Speaks* compete with other Black papers and even outrival certain very popular Black papers. We were seeing the Fruit of Islam in great numbers, hundreds of them on the streets of big cities like Chicago and New York and Los Angeles. We were seeing Malcolm on television frequently—in our eyes, defeating the opposition. A lot of things that were happening then were favoring our spirit and our hopes for the future.

Imam Wallace D. Mohammed

Louis X (now Farrakhan) (*left*) and others on platform at Nation of Islam rally, Harlem, early 1960s.

Malcolm X at Ronald Stokes funeral,
Los Angeles, May 1962.

Some other people had been shot, but Ronald Stokes was the only one who had died. Malcolm was furious, you know. He was furious. And I expected that particular moment something really explosive to take over.

Gordon Parks

The papers reported it as a shoot out. There's absolutely no question, I emphasize no question, that it was no shoot out. There was a policeman who had been injured, but that undoubtedly came from some ricochet from their weapon. The police charged into the mosque for no good reason, except they wanted to see what was in the mosque.

Stanley Malone

Malcolm X at Muslim assault trial, Los Angeles, May 3, 1963.

Malcolm was walking back and forth, shaking his head, saying, "They're gonna pay for it, they're gonna pay for it, they're gonna pay for it."

Gordon Parks

We flew back through Phoenix and Elijah Muhammad told Malcolm very definitely: If you had reacted the way you should have reacted, if you'd have had more faith in Allah, Ronald Stokes would be alive. That was it. He really gave him an upbraiding. And Malcolm said nothing. He just listened.

Gordon Parks

Malcolm's response was he wanted to do something about it. And naturally, Mr. Muhammad heard about it. He told Malcolm, "That's one man we lost. I never did tell you that we weren't going to lose anyone, or some, or a few. 'Cause that's the way it is when you're building a nation." He said, "If I send my followers out there to do battle with those people in L.A., either undercover or on top of the covers, they will get slaughtered, and I'm not going to do that." And Malcolm didn't like that.

Yusuf Shah

Elijah
Muhammad
at Nation of
Islam rally,
International
Amphitheater,
Chicago, 1962.

Malcolm felt sort of let down, and a lot of us did, so to speak, because we Muslims were people that said, "Never be the aggressor, but if someone attacks you, we do not teach you to turn the other cheek."

Benjamin Karim

Malcolm had made a statement about the plane full of people from Georgia that crashed—I think it was a hundred and eight people were killed on it. He said, God has answered our prayer. You know, that was a very ignorant thing for any kind of a leader to say. Elijah Muhammad got after him and admonished him good.

Abdul Aziz Omar

Malcolm X with part of the ruling family of the Nation of Islam, Clara Muhammad (*center*) and Ethel Sharrieff, daughter of Clara and Elijah Muhammad, 1961.

Nation of Islam officials Raymond Sharrieff, son-in-law of Elijah Muhammad
and Supreme Captain of the Fruit of Islam (*facing camera*), and John Ali,
national secretary (*far left*), Chicago, 1960s.

Malcolm began to talk less and less about how God was going to get rid of the Caucasians, and he began to talk about how we were gon' be able to go into court and bring them to justice, that they are guilty according to the law of the land—which was not our argument at all. Our argument was that we were a divine people and that we would be protected and finally delivered, put in the seat of authority by Allah. That was our teaching at that time.

Abdul Aziz Omar

Oh, Malcolm is fitting in, but he's changed. Changed from religious talk to nationalistic talk. To the point where I told him that I listened to him when he first started, and I listened to him now, and that I felt change. He said, "What kind of change you mean?" I said, "Well, your talks caused me to have chills, because of the truth that you were saying. Now I don't feel that anymore." "Well," he said, "maybe you have lost your religion or your spirit." I said, "Well, maybe I have. But I don't feel or hear it anymore in your talk."

Yusuf Shah

Muhammad Speaks
FREEDOM
CAN'T WAIT!
Truth Is The Best Guidance
Hits Slow Pace At Big Rally
Randolph Warns on

During that time, 1962, Malcolm had begun to suspect the national staff was complaining that his intentions were not all good. That he was building his own image and was working harder to promote his own image than he was to promote the image of the Nation of Islam or the message of the Honorable Elijah Muhammad. They were passing on this suspicion to members in the ministry and to captains and officers in the Fruit of Islam. They had begun to organize a great force to discredit and to put a check on Malcolm.

Imam Wallace D. Mohammed

Malcolm had to be heard south of a Hundred Twenty-fifth Street, had to be heard by a national audience, both of whites and Blacks. He understood that the most powerful instrument of communication then, as now, is television. It was at a more primitive state than it is now, but the way to be heard was to be able to say something in ten seconds or thirty seconds. Malcolm was, I think, the first master of the sound byte.

Peter Goldman

I think the general press thought of Malcolm as the central figure in the Muslims. It was impossible not to think so, 'cause his voice is being heard on the news every day, and he was the one who issued statements for the Muslim hierarchy. But he would always say, the Honorable Elijah Muhammad. He'd always put that first. He was very sensitive about that.

Gordon Parks

There had never been a discussion about a successor other than Wallace D. Muhammad. Mike Wallace named Malcolm the heir apparent—that was his words. But the only successor that ever was discussed in our community was Wallace D. Muhammad. He is Mr. Muhammad's biological son. And he is the successor. And only him.

Yusuf Shah

Malcolm X discusses "Race Relations in Crisis" on television. Rev. Wyatt Tee Walker, a chief aide to Rev. Dr. Martin Luther King, Jr., sits to Malcolm's left and James Farmer, director of CORE, with back to camera, 1963.

Malcolm X with group of young white people, 1961.

Malcolm X and Wallace D. Muhammad, son of Elijah Muhammad, 1961.

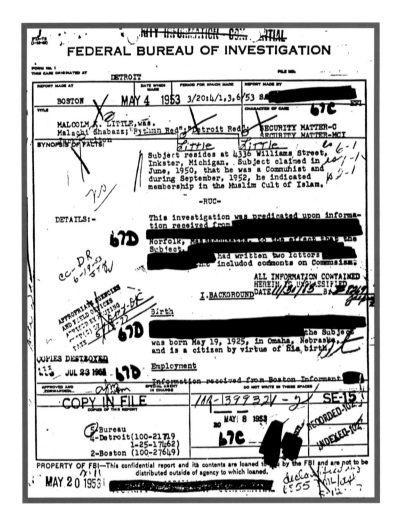

The first page in the FBI file on Malcolm X. It states the Bureau's reason—two letters in which Malcolm refers to communism—for opening its investigation.

Benjamin Karim stands behind Malcolm at a Nation of Islam rally, Washington, D.C., May 1963.

We didn't know it at the time, but we found as time has gone by, we can look at the FBI files now and see where they were ordered to take that thing and make a split out of it. The orders to the FBI was to bring about a split here.

Wilfred Little

I had heard that there were all kinds of means used to infiltrate the Muslims, to learn as much about them as they could. Of course, the police department uses people to get information, and they used every means they could.

Robert Mangum

Minister Malcolm was sitting in the Muslim restaurant in Queens. This is in 1963. He had his forehead buried in his hands, and he was sitting sideways on the stool. He looked miserable, and whenever he was concerned about something, he would pull his forehead together and you would see all these wrinkles. He told me, "You know, I just came from my doctor. I went to her because," he said, "my head was hurting me so bad that I thought my brain cells were bleeding."

Benjamin Karim

Nation of Islam members picket Criminal Courts Building, where two members stand trial on charges stemming from police harassment of *Muhammad Speaks* vendors in Times Square, New York, January 11, 1963.

The indiscretions that Elijah Muhammad had practiced were a known thing probably a year or more before Malcolm ever began to realize it, but the word was getting around all the time. When Malcolm finally found out, it made him sick. I tell you, it took him a while to regain his composure.

Wilfred Little

Times Square, February 13, 1963. Malcolm X leads a demonstration protesting police actions against Muslims in New York City and Rochester. Such a street protest in midtown Manhattan was unheard of for Muslims.

The Nation did to some extent contain everyone's activism, which was probably a little tragic. You'd get revved up and ready to go, but be restrained by the limitations of the philosophy and focus of the Nation of Islam. That was really a tremendous struggle for me personally. I was ready to go out and turn the world upside down, but that wasn't the program.

Amina Rahman

The Nation of Islam just wasn't ready for that. And Malcolm had a hard time holding himself in check because he felt like he was in a straitjacket. You could see that as time went by, it was gonna get worse. And it did, because he had a time staying in that straitjacket.

Wilfred Little

Above: Martin Luther King, Jr., and other leaders lock arms during the March on Washington, August 28, 1963.

Left: John Lewis (*left*) and James Zwerg, attacked after a "freedom ride," Montgomery, Alabama, May 20, 1961.

Rally in support of civil rights struggle in Mississippi, in front of National Memorial African Bookstore, Harlem, March 23, 1963. An effigy of Mississippi governor Ross Barnett hangs above Malcolm.

In Cambridge, Maryland, during the course of the movement, I found that most of the people we were organizing had heard of Malcolm X and respected him. And listened to him any time he was going to be on. They made an effort to hear those speeches and felt that he understood what their problems were and that they needed to be fought against. And, I suppose, not always nonviolently.

Gloria Richardson

We were willing to listen to Malcolm because, on one hand, Malcolm inspired us. Malcolm said things in New York, in Chicago, around the country, that maybe some people in the South and in other parts of the country didn't have the courage to say.

John Lewis

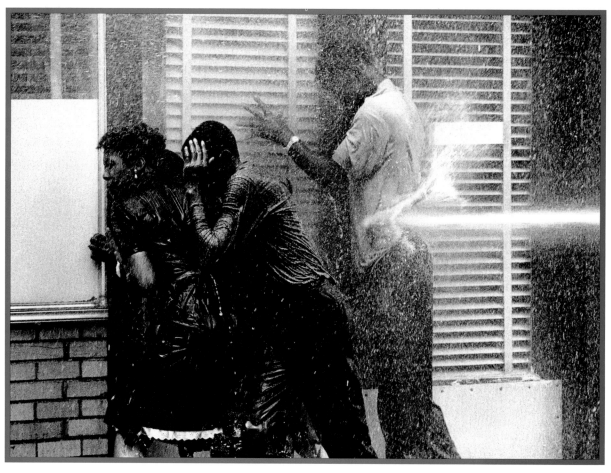

I got a copy of John Lewis's speech. He was chairman of SNCC at that time and was scheduled to speak at the March on Washington, but had written a speech that many considered inflammatory—he was forbidden to give his original speech. I felt like I was carrying contraband. When I showed it to Malcolm, he told me he wanted me to read it at the next Saturday rally. I was excited, but really puzzled. Women from the Nation of Islam stood upstairs in the temple and watched the rallies out the window. I was trying to figure out, am I gonna read this speech from the window? And Malcolm said, "No, of course, you're gonna sit on the platform with me. Get up and read your speech, and then just sit there." I knew that despite what he said during lectures in the temple, Malcolm didn't think I should be upstairs behind the curtain either.

Amina Rahman

The bombing that Sunday morning in Birmingham was one of those things that would happen that would bring people out to the temple in droves to hear what Malcolm had to say about it. The radio said that four children had been killed, and my thoughts were immediately sadness, rage, confusion—and then, *I gotta hear what Malcolm says about it.*

Amina Rahman

The mood in Harlem was one of just tremendous anger and frustration. It was almost as bad as when the boy was shot the next summer, causing the Harlem uprising. I think that easily could have happened. And without Brother Malcolm, it may have happened. But he was not a believer in spontaneous action. It was his position that the police would deliberately try to bring about certain things, to smoke certain people out. So Malcolm's thing was, "Don't be a part of what you didn't start."

Peter Bailey

A lot of us became dissatisfied. And I think Malcolm became dissatisfied. We weren't doing anything to help our people who were being brutalized by the whites and the police. We wanted to send some brothers down to Birmingham to train Black people to fight.

Benjamin Karim

Opposite page: *above*, Harlem, May 15, 1963. A large crowd gathers to hear Malcolm X speak in support of civil rights struggle in Birmingham, Alabama; *below*, Birmingham, Alabama, 1963. Demonstrators are hosed by firemen.

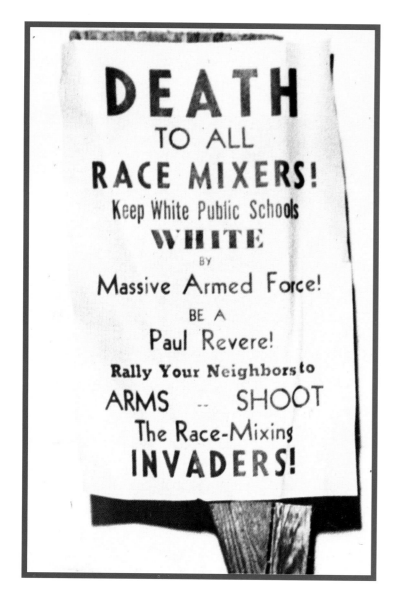

Dummy rifle and sign planted in yards of liberals in several Florida cities, winter 1959–60.

I think there's always been a dread among white people of what's been called the Black revenge. Our relations with our Black population have always been quite neurotic, and part of the neurosis is the sense that someday these people who have been oppressed so long are going to exact a terrible revenge. To hear this guy stand on television and talk about white devils and later about guns, even though he was talking about self-defense, I think was quite frightening.

Peter Goldman

In my opinion, the "Message to the Grass Roots," a speech made by Malcolm X in Detroit, was singularly the finest revolutionary message delivered by a Black man in the twentieth century. What he is saying is that land is the basis of nation. That when people take the land away from you, they take away not only your nationhood, they take away your humanhood, your manhood, your womanhood, the essence of your being. Until you regain the land, you have no discussion about nation, because without the land, there can be no nation.

John Henrik Clarke

John F. Kennedy had been assassinated that Thursday. Mr. Muhammad had his son call Malcolm at the mosque on Friday. He said, "My father said that we should say that we are sorry about the death of our president." After we hung up the phone, Malcolm turned to me and said, "How can I say that? After what I have been saying?" My response to Malcolm was that I don't see why we can't say that, because this is what our instructions were. He said, "Well, you just don't understand." From then on, his problems began.

Yusuf Shah

Ad from *Muhammad Speaks*, November 22, 1963. Malcolm X spoke at the December 1 meeting in place of Elijah Muhammad.

APPEARING IN PERSON ... IN NEW YORK CITY

The Honorable

ELIJAH MUHAMMAD

MESSENGER OF ALLAH

SPEAKS

IN NEW YORK CITY

SUNDAY •• DECEMBER 1st

Hear This All-Important Message at

Manhattan Center

34th STREET and 8th AVE., NEW YORK CITY

DOORS OPEN 1 P.M.

ADMISSION FREE

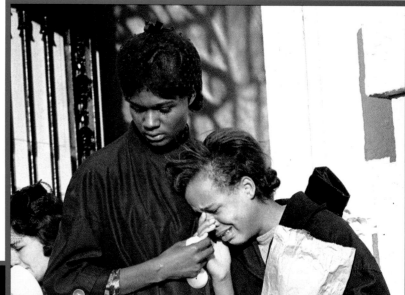

Great Rotunda, Capitol,
Washington, D.C.,
November 24, 1963.
Women mourn the
death of President
John F. Kennedy.

Harlem, May 15,
1963. Malcolm X
addresses rally in
support of civil
rights struggle in
Birmingham,
Alabama.

That Friday night, the temple was packed. Malcolm talked for hours. In his skillful way, his whole talk was about the Kennedy assassination, but I don't think he ever mentioned the name once. It foreshadowed what he would do in the speech on Sunday, December first. He had been directed not to say any more than that he was shocked at the assassination. So he did something that he never did before: He had a prepared speech. He was clearly nervous about what he might say. But then, as if courting disaster, he opened up the floor to questions.

Amina Rahman

When Minister Malcolm made the statement about the chickens coming home to roost, it was an answer to a question asked by a lady in the audience. But John Ali was at the meeting, and they were trying to find some way to get rid of Minister Malcolm. They thought that Mr. Muhammad was going to die from this bronchitis. When John Ali went back to Chicago and told Mr. Muhammad that Malcolm had made this statement, then Malcolm was suspended for ninety days.

Benjamin Karim

It was reported as though he was almost, you know, jumping up and down and clicking his heels, and some Black people who had begun to listen to what he was saying found themselves being horrified that he would make such a statement. That was a setback to Brother Malcolm in terms of reaching the Black community.

Peter Bailey

The headlines were there, and the characterization of his speech was there, and he was in real hot water in the Nation of Islam. He had done exactly what he and Elijah Muhammad had cautioned everybody not to do. He had made a substantial comment on Kennedy's assassination in a way that put the Nation of Islam in trouble. So he had to pay for that.

Amina Rahman

FIGHTING
ON THREE
FRONTS

Much of the focus on Malcolm X's last year has tended to be on his trip to Mecca, his conversion to "true Islam," and his "change of heart" concerning white people. What is underappreciated is that Malcolm's reaching out to nonracist whites was part of a general pattern of outreach and experimentation as he sought to heal wounds and forge alliances to be

Opposite: Cairo mosque,
August 1964.

more effective in his struggle to reform American racial practices. Only the uneasy and the self-absorbed want to dwell exclusively on Malcolm's "coming to his senses," as though he now unconditionally forgave America its racial sins. But Malcolm was not into meaningless forgiveness. (Remember, he planned to take the United States before the United Nations to charge it with genocide.) Rather, Malcolm was seeking a rational way out of America's racist maze. His zigs and zags simply conformed to the convolutions of The Problem.

What he deeply believed—answering a question once posed by the French writer and philosopher Albert Camus: Can a system condemn itself?—was that America would never willingly and peacefully change. He believed that Blacks, only by mustering whatever allies they could inside the country, and bolstered by African and Third World allies outside the country, could pry freedom and equality out of the racist closet into which they had been so long sequestered. But before he could get to that stage, Malcolm had to get his own political-religious house in order.

AMBIVALENCE AND INDEPENDENCE

After the reprimand of December 4, Malcolm pursued a policy of noticeable ambivalence toward the Nation. He continued working on the *Autobiography* with Alex Haley, and he did nothing to impede the news stories flowing out of the *Amsterdam News* and other papers. Most egregiously, he accepted an invitation from Muhammad Ali (then Cassius Clay) to visit Miami where Clay was in training to fight Sonny Liston for the heavyweight championship of the world. Joining Clay's camp kept Malcolm highly visible without technically being disobedient. But since he did talk to sports reporters about the religious symbolism of the fight, his behavior was not what one might have expected from someone supposedly acting out the penance of contrition. Privately, however, he had sent a humble appeal for reinstatement to Elijah Muhammad: "If you would have mercy upon me and give me another chance, I'd stay out of the public. I'd be satisfied to just minister in the mosque, making no public statements nor outside speeches."

Malcolm had gone to Miami less than two weeks after he had been summoned to Phoenix in January and told "to put out the fire you've started" (about Muhammad's transgressions). Elijah Muhammad had also told him that he was no longer the National Representative of the Nation of Islam nor the minister of Temple No. 7. Now Malcolm probably saw the handwriting on the wall. Indeed, after the Phoenix meeting, the punching and counterpunching became fast and furious.

On February 15, Muhammad publicly disinvited Malcolm from participating in the Savior's Day Convention in Chicago on February 26. On February 17, Malcolm wrote Elijah Muhammad requesting clarification of his status. On February 21, Elijah's secretary telephoned Malcolm to reaffirm the ninety-day suspension and to deny Malcolm's request for a hearing on the charges against him. On February 22, a story appeared in the *Amsterdam News* to the effect that Malcolm would return to action "whether his suspension is lifted or not." On March 5, Malcolm received word from Muhammad that he had been suspended for "an indefinite period of time." On March 8, chickens "came home to roost" for Malcolm X. He announced that he was leaving the Nation. "I am going to organize and head a new Mosque in New York City known as the Muslim Mosque, Inc. This will give us a religious base, and the spiritual force necessary to rid our people of the vices that destroy the moral fiber of our community."

It is rumored that when Elijah Muhammad heard that Malcolm had left him, he cried.

Evidently the grief did not last long or turned quickly into get-evenness, because two days after Malcolm's declaration of independence, he received a certified letter demanding that he return all property of the Nation's within his possession—including his home in East Elmhurst! The Nation's divestment act set in motion a chain of legal struggles, including eviction proceedings, that would be fought out in the courts throughout 1964 and symbolize the acrimony that now characterized the relationship between Malcolm and the Nation.

Vilified in *Muhammad Speaks*, hounded by death threats, accused of being "a hypocrite" (the Black Muslim equivalent to a Catholic who commits mortal sin), Malcolm would be followed, harassed, and physically menaced by the Nation until his death. Thus his achievements during this last year must be considered all the more significant since they were accomplished in the face of the ongoing necessity to fight a very personal battle of defense in behalf of himself and his still-growing family. (He and Betty now had four daughters.)

Malcolm also had to carve out a niche for himself in the freedom struggle that clearly distinguished him from his past with the Nation. Nor would it be enough to simply declare himself a changed man. He had made too many enemies for it to be that simple. What Malcolm needed was a new spiritual base for himself and those Muslims who wanted to follow him. And he also needed to be welcomed into the fellowship of the real Islam. That is why he started his own mosque, why he had been studying orthodox Islam, and why he borrowed money from his sister Ella to make an April pilgrimage to Mecca, the hajj.

In the month prior to his departure for the Middle East, though, Malcolm made a number of moves to establish a new political image on a par with what he was trying to do spiritually.

First he became a supporting member of the federation of urban Black community leaders called ACT, pulled together by Jesse Gray, the Harlem rent-strike leader. This group represented the most militant community-based element of the Black left in the urban North and included such activists as Julius Hobson from Washington, D.C., Gloria Richardson from Cambridge, Maryland, Stanley Branche from Chester, Pennsylvania, Lawrence Landry and Nahaz Rogers from Chicago, as well as Jesse Gray and others. Malcolm associated himself with ACT two days after founding Muslim Mosque, Inc. (MMI), and he spoke at a rent strike rally organized by Jesse Gray shortly afterwards. He also supported the New York City school boycott led by Reverend Milton Galamison of Brooklyn. Thus Malcolm had taken specific steps to associate himself with two of the most pressing secular problems afflicting urban Black America: housing and education.

In another move, unthinkable in his Black Muslim period, Malcolm went to Washington to monitor Senate debate on the Civil Rights Bill then being filibustered against! Malcolm, even peripherally related to support for civil rights, was a revolutionary development the press seemed unable to relate to. As Malcolm complained subsequently to Alex Haley: "They won't let me turn the corner."

Dr. Martin Luther King was also in the Senate that day. The two men ran into each other and posed for a picture, which is the only one we have of them together.

Before leaving for Mecca, then, Malcolm had sent out unmistakable signals of a new beginning. He had totally abandoned the traditional Black Muslim position of noninvolvement in civic and political affairs in favor of supporting mass-based attempts to alleviate the day-to-day problems besetting Black people. His new flexibility even included giving the "devils'" law a respectful hearing.

Thus the "new Malcolm" had made his appearance before Mecca. He had reached out to nonreligious constituencies and tried to mend fences. The trip to Saudi Arabia now afforded Malcolm the opportunity to try and mend the highest fence of all: his categorical rejection of all whites as devils.

MALCOLM AND WHITE AMERICANS

Commenting on his hajj, Malcolm wrote back to his supporters in America and to M. S. Handler, a senior white reporter on the *New York Times* whom he had come to like, that the experience had impressed him with: ". . . The brotherhood! The people of all races, colors, from all over the world coming together as one! It has proved to me the power of the One God."

Some critics have seen Malcolm's sudden reversal as a "public relations ploy" but they fail to give sufficient weight to the fact that Malcolm made an important distinction between white Christian America and a white, potentially Islamic America.

Malcolm's "new" attitude was not unconditional acceptance of *existing* America. Rather he raised the possibility of human brotherhood between the races if white Americans accepted "the Oneness of God" under Islam and effected a moral and spiritual reformation. The other possible force for change, Malcolm suggested, lay in the young whites he had met in the colleges and universities. He felt they might "turn to the spiritual path of truth—the only way left to America to ward off the disaster that racism must inevitably lead to."

It is true that Malcolm had been to the Middle East before and undoubtedly seen white Muslims before without coming to this new revelation. But in 1959, he was not ready to equate American whites with white Muslims abroad. Recall his observation about the blizzard of calls he received after *The Hate That Hate Produced* documentary. Malcolm noted that Europeans were never as defensive as American whites: "One funny thing—in all that hectic period, something quickly struck my notice: The Europeans never pressed the 'hate' question. Only the American white man was so plagued and obsessed with being 'hated.'" In Malcolm's mind American white people were a special case with a special set of problems that only Allah and/or significant non-white political power could solve. But Malcolm's reflections on the possibilities of cooperation with reformed white Americans raises an important and rarely considered question: What was Malcolm X's potential in regard to leading whites? That danger was certainly as profound as Malcolm's cause being taken up in the United Nations by sympathetic African states. The latter would be an embarrassment; the former might lead to revolution.

DECLARING WAR ABROAD

Malcolm's five weeks abroad in the Middle East and Africa are extraordinary in the way that they reconfirm his unique ability to impact upon persons of other races, languages, and cultures. Unable to speak Arabic, he yet impressed the Muslims with whom he could not converse; a commoner, he was treated like royalty by Prince Faysal, ruler of Saudi Arabia; an American so-called hate-monger, he was yet granted an audience with Dr. Kwame Nkrumah, president of Ghana, and warmly embraced by the Ghanaian and Nigerian students before whom he spoke. That Malcolm was able to make such an impression on so wide a variety of people from different stations in life is a tribute once again to those marvelous personal qualities that had made him such a successful architect of the Nation of Islam.

Malcolm returned with a new Islamic name, El-Hajj Malik El-Shabazz, and also with one bestowed upon him in Nigeria, Alhadji Omowale (in Yoruba "the child has come home"). Paradoxically, Malcolm, struggling to reposition himself amidst the competing currents of the Black struggle in America, seems to have been accepted by the leaders of Middle Eastern and African states as *the* Negro leader. No longer the emissary of the Honorable Elijah Muhammad, but the putative ambassador of Black America, Malcolm sought and, according to him, received pledges from some of the new African nations to charge the United States in the United Nations with state discrimination against Black Americans.

Malcolm probably had two plans in mind when he left the country: to become accepted as a bona fide Muslim and thence establish ties with the Arab states on the basis of religion and to establish similar ties with African states on the basis of race. But either the trip radicalized Malcolm or he had something more politically specific in mind all the while than just making the hajj. One talk he gave at the University of Ghana, "Will Africa Ignite America's Racial Powder Keg?," for example, links perfectly with his specific proposal to charge the United States with genocide at the UN: "How can you [the African nations in the U.N.] condemn Portugal and South Africa while our Black people are being bitten by dogs and beaten with clubs?"

But by threatening to embarrass the United States in such a fashion, Malcolm invigorated a second front against himself; the State and Justice Departments joined the crowd that considered Malcolm a danger.

Candidly, one of their spokesmen told the *New York Times*: "If Malcolm X succeeds in convincing just one African government to bring up the charge at the United Nations, the United States would be faced with a touchy problem." And if this brazenness was not enough to upset America's cold warriors, Malcolm was roundly feted in Africa by the Cubans, the Algerians (fresh from the triumph of their eight-year revolution), and the Red Chinese.

Fighting on two fronts, *against* the conservatism of the Nation of Islam and *for* the liberation of Black America, Malcolm did not realize the extent to which a covert war, a third front, was being waged against him—and Martin Luther King—as it had been waged against Black America for more than half a century.

AN ASIDE: THE FBI VS. BLACK AMERICA

Not until 1975, ten years after Malcolm's assassination and King's march from Selma to Montgomery, in the wake of Watergate, did the Senate Select Committee on Intelligence (the Church Committee) reveal that elements of the CIA, the IRS, the NSA, army intelligence, and especially the FBI had perceived the freedom movement as an enemy.

In the most scurrilous of these counterintelligence programs (COINTELPRO) the FBI had bugged and burgled, blackmailed and wiretapped, slandered and connived, fabricated and intrigued, to bring the movement, and especially its leaders, down. In the Committee's own words, the FBI had "waged a secret and nation-wide war to destroy Martin Luther King and the Black Panther Party." But Martin and the Panthers were not the only Black targets of the FBI. It monitored the NAACP, ordered investigations of "every Black student union or similar group," and had opened a file on Malcolm in 1953.

That the FBI considered itself at war was made abundantly clear by a memorandum J. Edgar Hoover sent to all of his field offices in August 1964:

> "The news media of recent months mirror the civil rights issue
> as probably the number one issue in the political spectrum.
> There are clear and unmistakable signs that we are in the midst
> of a social revolution with the racial movement at its core. The
> Bureau, in meeting its responsibilities in this area, is an integral
> part of this revolution."

What Hoover couldn't say officially was that the Bureau would continue to play the counterrevolutionary role it had carved out for itself long since, a role that brought it into conflict with Black people in general and with Malcolm X in particular.

BACK TO THE NATION

Fired up by his reception in Africa, Malcolm returned to America and quickly went about fashioning the more politically oriented Organization of Afro-American Unity (OAAU) as a sister organization to its role model, the Organization of African Unity (OAU), and its predecessor, the Muslim Mosque, Inc.

The OAAU charter spoke of the Black right of self-defense and of Black people controlling their own destiny, and it pledged itself to fight for unity, promote justice, and "transcend compromise."

But these new political developments did not prevent the Nation from pressing its assaults against Malcolm. Eviction hearings were scheduled and postponed. Muslims around the country, including his brother Philbert, a minister, denounced him, and threatening phone calls were made to his home. False rumors were also circulated about him. Reaching the end of his tether, Malcolm struck back. He went public on radio and television about Mr. Muhammad being "the father of six illegitimate children."

Curiously, though Malcolm's allegations were supported by paternity suits filed in Los Angeles by two of Mr. Muhammad's former secretaries, and though Mr. Muhammad's sons, Wallace and Akbar, repudiated him, the mainstream press treated the revelations lightly and ignored the opportunity to destroy the Nation. It is difficult not to conclude that the powers that be did not consider Elijah Muhammad and the Nation anything approximating the threat posed by Malcolm as an individual.

In late June, Malcolm made another effort to calm the waters. He published an open letter in the *New York Post* calling for peace between Muhammad and himself. But it was much too late. Too much mud-slinging had been done, too much bad blood had been spilled, too much dirty laundry had been aired in public.

HARLEM VS. THE HOMELAND

On July 2, hurrying to finalize the document he planned to disseminate at the OAU meeting in Cairo in mid-July, Malcolm nevertheless paused to send telegrams to Martin Luther King and James Forman of SNCC offering "to send brothers" south to protect their civil rights workers and "give the KKK a taste of their own medicine." Malcolm was responding to the disappearance in Mississippi of the young men working on SNCC's and CORE's "Freedom Summer" project and the terrorizing of King-led demonstrators in St. Augustine by white vigilantes. The offer was not only ill-considered since he had no troops to send, it also highlighted a trap into which Malcolm seems to have fallen during this period of his life.

In his prime, Malcolm built the Nation from the ground up through his personal touch, quietly and off camera. He was on the streets, "fishing" outside Christian churches, holding small meetings in homes, and so forth. But from the time that *The Hate That Hate Produced* was telecast, Malcolm began to depend more and more on the press to do his organizing for him. (He was so effective in Africa because he reverted to his old style and because, on the continent, the American press was not the medium of his message. Thus Africans could get Malcolm, even through their own press, unfiltered, in a way American audiences could not.)

But in this last period, beset by a hundred problems, with no organizational apparatus like the one he had in the Nation to do his bidding, with a fourth child just born, and with a hundred brilliant ideas germinating in his head daily, but no time to do much more than react to life, Malcolm began to spend too much time organizing by press conference, through headline-making. That kept him in the news, but it did not build an organization. Moreover, he was announcing his ideas before they were fully formed, supported, or even in place, thereby telegraphing his moves and leaving himself open for checkmate and/or subversion. As potentially earth-shattering politically as his UN plan was, pursuing it took him out of Harlem and out of the country at the precise moment when the OAAU needed his leadership and at the precise moment when Harlem, and then Bedford-Stuyvesant, exploded over the shooting death of fifteen-year-old James Powell by off-duty police officer Thomas Gilligan.

The New York police deployed twenty-five thousand men to keep Harlem and Bed-Stuy in check. But Black New York was in a fury for three days, raging across boroughs, shouting "Killer cops must go!" Mayor Robert Wagner desperately sent for Martin Luther King, but the people hooted King down. Instead they cried "We want Malcolm." But Malcolm was away, pursuing a different agenda and audience.

The irony was that Malcolm's long-standing critique that nonviolence wouldn't work and was not really respected by the Black masses had been proven correct. The Prophet's warnings about mass rebellion had come true. But the Prophet was off pursuing another vision, and he was being perceived as failing Harlem that summer. The radical time—vouchsafed by the next half-decade of urban rebellions, nearly all precipitated by incidents with the police—had come. But the quintessential nationalist was away on a far-off continent, foreign-politicking. This damaged Malcolm's credibility far more than any character assassination by the Nation of Islam.

Later Malcolm would admit that his plan did not catch fire, but he blamed the people rather than his strategy:

> "I must be honest. Negroes—Afro-Americans—showed no inclination to rush to the United Nations and demand justice for themselves here in America. I really had known in advance that they wouldn't. The American white man has so thoroughly brainwashed the black man to see himself as only a domestic "civil rights" problem that it will probably take longer than I live before the Negro sees that the struggle of the American black man is international."

After six weeks at home, he flew back to Africa and spent almost five months there visiting fourteen countries and speaking with seven heads of state. Warning the Africans against America, including the Peace Corps, he explained his plan to take the United States before the World Court.

The tour was a personal and propaganda triumph. And in the United Nations African delegates did subsequently chastise the United States for being indifferent to the fate of Blacks everywhere, citing Mississippi as an example. But that New York criticism was not very much help to the "disappeared" young freedom fighters, one Black and two white, whom Malcolm had symbolically offered to help. They turned up dead: murdered in Philadelphia, Mississippi, by law officers and their Klan cohorts. J. Edgar Hoover, true to character, said that the FBI could not protect civil rights workers. He meant, of course, that they would not.

So Malcolm's significant advance in Pan-African foreign policy had had little immediate bearing on the destruction of southern, or northern, racism. But he continued to seek the political Holy Grail.

He supported the social reform efforts of the antipoverty agency in Harlem, HARYOU-ACT; he supported the Mississippi Freedom Democratic Party's challenge against Mississippi representatives elected because of Black voter exclusion; he spoke to young Black Mississippians from McComb (and their young German volunteer worker, who has never forgotten the experience); he spoke at the forums of the Socialist Workers Party; and he began more and more to talk about revolution in general and "The Black Revolution" in particular. In late December, in fact, he introduced to Harlem Abdul Mohammed Rahman Babu, a Tanzanian revolutionary Malcolm had met on the Africa trip. He was still struggling, trying to find "the answer"—and he was still traveling at that frantic, driven pace.

THE LAST DAYS AND THE LEGACY

Malcolm flew back to Europe in December to debate at Oxford and to speak in Paris to an admiring Malcolm X Committee that had been formed out of an earlier stay.

In early February he flew to Alabama at SNCC's invitation to speak at his wife Betty's old alma mater, Tuskegee. While in the state, SNCC invited him to come over to Selma, to Brown Chapel A.M.E. Church, to speak in support of the voting rights project SNCC and Dr. King's organization, the Southern Christian Leadership Conference (SCLC), were conducting.

King was in jail for leading demonstrations, so Malcolm agreed to come to express solidarity with him. The possibility that Malcolm, SNCC, and King might come together was truly alarming to the anti-Black forces in the government. An even more dire prospect was that Malcolm might lure away King's constituency with his radical northern nationalism. Coincidentally, a demonstration that had been scheduled for the day Malcolm was in Selma and in which he might, therefore, have participated, was canceled. Malcolm thereupon flew back to New York and then on to London to speak at the London School of Economics. From there he flew to Paris to speak to a group of African students but he was barred from entering France by the French government. So he came home.

When he returned to America this time, the end was near. On February 14 his home was firebombed, and on February 21, Malcolm was murdered in a fusillade of bullets in the Audubon Ballroom. The one man who has confessed to the crime has said that the two men convicted with him are innocent and that the true circumstances of Malcolm's assassination have yet to come out. But the authorities have adopted their Dallas-JFK posture and cling to the official story.

Malcolm was dead, but the conjunction of history and Malcolm's philosophy created more disciples than he ever knew. These men and women ushered in the Age of Black Power that followed Malcolm's death, because Malcolm's travels that built the Nation built Malcolm's non-Nation following too. In destroying the illusion that the North was somehow "different," Malcolm helped create the conditions to theorize about race as a national problem and therefore to conceive of America differently. And he was heard.

Amiri Baraka (LeRoi Jones) and the late writer and critic Larry Neal heard him and called for a Black Arts Movement. Stokely Carmichael (Kwame Turé), attending the Bronx High School of Science, heard him. Milton Henry and his brother, Richard, in Detroit, heard him and asked Malcolm to run for the Senate in Michigan in 1964 on the all-Black Freedom Now Party. (Later Richard Henry became president of the Republic of New Africa, which tried to implement the Muslim call for land and nationhood in five southern states. They bought land in Mississippi, but quickly had a shoot-out with the FBI and Mississippi police—so their dream came to naught. But the name of their intended capital in the New Republic was to have been Malik.)

Two Oakland youths heard Malcolm and formed the Black Panther Party for Self-Defense (against police brutality). They also adopted Malcolm's United Nations plan in modified form as part of their Ten Point Program. Ron Everett heard him, created the political-cultural organization US, and became Maulana Ron Karenga, creator of the popular African American holiday observance, Kwanzaa. James Baldwin heard him and wrote *The Fire Next Time*. SNCC, disillusioned with white liberals, the FBI, President Lyndon B. Johnson, and the Democratic party, heard him and called for "Black Power." Adam Clayton Powell, at whose church Malcolm often spoken, heard him and convened the First Black Power Conference. And poet Don L. Lee heard him and became activist writer and publisher Haki Madhubuti.

There is, in short, hardly a Black man or woman over forty-five who heard Malcolm X and went unaffected by the hearing. Because, as Peter Bailey, a Malcolm lieutenant in the OAAU, says, "Even if you didn't agree with him, Malcolm made you rethink your position."

That is the answer to the question someone foolishly asked years ago:

What did Malcolm X ever do for Black people? Not very much. He only gave us that small gift without which these words, and the deeds to which they are kin, would be quite inconceivable: He gave us the Black perspective.

Malcolm lives today in the hopes of people yearning for authentic heroes. Malcolm lives today because there is a new racism and because the old problems have not gone away, and if they are faced honestly, they will, over time, radicalize the best of us:

> ". . . I have found out that all I have been doing in trying to correct this system in America has been in vain . . . I am trying to get to the roots of it to see just what ought to be done . . . The whole thing will have to be done away with."

> —Martin Luther King, Jr., November 11, 1967

In Their Own Words

Osman Ahmed — Friend; met Malcolm X while a student at Dartmouth

Prince Mohmaed Al-Faysal — Crown Prince of Saudi Arabia

Muhammad Ali — Formerly Cassius Clay, member of the Nation of Islam

Maya Angelou — Writer; friend and associate from Africa trips

Peter Bailey — Journalist; member of OAAU

Stokely Carmichael — Member of SNCC, now Kwame Turé

John Henrik Clarke — Historian; member of OAAU

Ella Collins — half sister of Malcolm X

Ossie Davis — Friend; actor and activist

Muriel Feelings — Member of OAAU

Peter Goldman — Journalist

Alex Haley — Coauthor of *The Autobiography of Malcolm X*

Benjamin Karim — Close associate of Malcolm X in the Nation of Islam and Muslim Mosque, Inc.

Yuri Kochiyama — Harlem community activist; associate of Malcolm X

John Lewis — Member of SNCC

Robert Little — Malcolm X's half brother

Wilfred Little — Malcolm X's eldest brother

Imam Wallace D. Mohammed — Son of Elijah Muhammad

Abdul Aziz Omar — Formerly Philbert Little, Malcolm X's elder brother

Gordon Parks — *Life* photographer

Amina Rahman — Formerly Sharon X, joined Nation of Islam as a teenager; close associate of Malcolm X

Gloria Richardson — Civil rights leader in Cambridge, Maryland; associate of Malcolm X

Gene Roberts — N.Y.P.D. officer who infiltrated the OAAU as an undercover agent

Sonia Sanchez — Writer; member of N.Y. CORE

Cleveland Sellers — Program secretary of SNCC

Attallah Shabazz — Malcolm X's eldest daughter

Yusuf Shah — Formerly Captain Joseph, Fruit of Islam, Mosque No. 7

Percy Sutton — Noted Harlem leader and N.Y. assemblyman; Malcolm X's lawyer

Alice Windom — Friend and associate of Malcolm X in Africa

Yvonne Woodward — Malcolm X's younger sister

Malcolm with Muhammad Ali and Lewis Michaux,
proprietor of the National Memorial African Bookstore on
125th Street, Harlem, February 26, 1964.

My first impression was how could a Black man talk about the government,
white people, and act so bold, and not be shot at? Talking about just a whole
movement, totally different from others, and so bold. How could he say these
things? Only God must be protecting him.

Muhammad Ali

Elijah Muhammad terms President Kennedy's death "tragic" and prints a "correction" of Malcolm's December 1 statement on the front page of *Muhammad Speaks*, December 20, 1963. He asserts that Malcolm "was speaking for himself and not for the Muslims in general."

As I look back on it now, years later, I can see how Elijah Muhammad could be very nervous about the chickens come home to roost statement and want to distance himself from it. The Nation of Islam, probably rightfully so, feared that a statement of this type would give the government an opportunity to smash them. I would say now that Brother Malcolm, with his knowledge of how the press operates, probably should not have said that.

Peter Bailey

Shiloh Baptist Church, Harlem, March, 1964. In an article on President Kennedy in *Muhammad Speaks*, December 20, 1963, Elijah Muhammad refers to Malcolm X as "still a great worker and Minister of ours . . . I do not classify Minister Malcolm as a hypocrite . . ."

If Elijah Muhammad died and Malcolm X took over the Nation, the first thing he might do was some serious housecleaning. He would move the moneychangers out of the temple. So the idea was to get rid of him before the event of the passing of the old man.

John Henrik Clarke

In the temple, we were being told Malcolm had done something terrible, that we couldn't be told in detail what it was, and that we shared in the blame for all of the above. That was a lot to take.

Amina Rahman

In Islam, when you are considered a hypocrite, it's quite different than in Christianity or politics or even just posing as a friend. In Islam, such as with the threats on Salman Rushdie, there is a possibility that that charge can cause you to be killed by those who are believers.

Benjamin Karim

He began in late 1963 to work with me—attending meetings in my political club and being seen with me out on the street. He helped me register voters and make telephone calls. In Albany, people were wondering, "Who is this guy, Percy Sutton, bringing in that revolutionary Malcolm X?" But that was the first thought. Then came the conservative Republicans and conservative Democrats who wanted to take a picture with Minister Malcolm, wanted to shake his hand. He was a celebrity.

Percy Sutton

Going to Florida, for my family, was a honeymoon. My parents referred to it as a honeymoon. For us children it was an opportunity to be with each other on a plane and the adventures of that. But as my mother and father talked about it, it was the first time in their marital life that they had time for themselves, where he was not being, twenty-four–seven, a public servant.

Attallah Shabazz

On the steps of the State Building, Malcolm X is flanked by his friend and attorney, Percy Sutton (*right*), Charles Rangel (*left*), and others, after Sutton's election to the State Assembly, Albany, New York, 1964.

Malcolm snaps Cassius Clay at his training camp, Miami, February 1964.

I was really shocked, but Malcolm, in his travels, sent postal cards. I have one here from Florida with two monkeys on it. It says "Negro leaders"—underscored—"could learn something from these monkeys, who have more freedom in America than Negroes do, and those monkeys haven't had to wait for civil rights legislation. Maybe our leaders should let these monkeys lead us. Brother Malcolm X."

Gloria Richardson

I met Malcolm quite a number of times at the Islamic center on Riverside Drive. After the prayers he used to sit down with me and Dr. Mahmoud Shawarbi, the director of the center, and talk about different aspects of Islam, since we thought their beliefs in the Nation of Islam were incorrect. So his association with orthodox Muslims in fact started much earlier than his pilgrimage to Mecca.

Osman Ahmed

I showed up for my job at the *Muhammad Speaks* office and was told I wasn't needed anymore. A couple of nights later, I went out to teach one of the classes for women at the Nation. Someone else was teaching my class. You didn't get paid for a lot of these jobs, but you got certain privileges, and one was not having to pay for meals in the restaurant, within reason. I went there to eat and signed my check, and the waiter brought it back to me and said, "I'm sorry, sister, you'll have to pay for this."

Amina Rahman

I was still in the Nation of Islam when Malcolm released the information to the *Amsterdam News* about this brother being sent to place a bomb in his car. Matter of fact, I used that article and that incident as a way to leave the Nation of Islam. They had been using articles against Malcolm that were in the white media, and the article about the bomb was in the Black newspaper. They said these were all lies. So I said, in front of everybody in the temple, if I can believe what white newspapers say about Minister Malcolm, then surely I can believe what a Black newspaper says about this brother.

Benjamin Karim

One couple, they hadn't been married very long; both were officials in Temple No. 7. He went to hear Malcolm speak at a meeting, to hear Malcolm's side of the story. When that became known at the mosque, his name went up on a list of people who were no longer in good standing with the mosque. He went home, and his wife said, "Choose! Malcolm, or the Nation and me." He chose Malcolm, and she threw all of his clothes out the window.

Amina Rahman

Malcolm lends support to local political battles just after leaving the Nation of Islam. He poses with public school boycott leaders Rev. Milton Galamison (*left*) and Rep. Adam Clayton Powell, Harlem, March 16, 1964.

Philbert X (*left*) denounces his "wayward" brother Malcolm, Chicago, March 26, 1964.

The incident with Mr. Muhammad and the secretaries, believe it or not, did not bother us as much as the corruption that we saw among the officials. There were many others from all over this country that left the Nation of Islam because of that. The Sunday that I left, a lot of Muslims left, not because of me, but because they were already dissatisfied. And I think that's something that should be understood.

Benjamin Karim

There is nothing ever hurt Malcolm like Elijah Muhammad dumping him.

Abdul Aziz Omar

Mr. Muhammad woulda give him the house. He wasn't opposed to that. But when Malcolm began to speak like he was speaking, after he left the community, Mr. Muhammad said, "Well, why should we reward him?" He said, "Brother, who owns that house?" "Well, we own it. The community owns it." He said, "Are you sure?" I said, "Yes." He said, "Well, it's ours, then." And that's why we went to court.

Yusuf Shah

For me, the continuity, and the image and the energy in my house, was very much the same. Those ill energies were replaced by more positive people.

Attallah Shabazz

Opposite page: New York, 1964.

When Malcolm left the Nation of Islam, I think there was some tension within the family. Mainly because we didn't talk candidly about some of the things that may have triggered his leaving and some of the behaviors of some of my family relative to his leaving. In 1972, I saw a movie. And for the first time, I saw my brother reading a very negative statement about Malcolm. It hurt me, it shocked me, it appalled me. And I think I will have many years to come before I would ever accept the fact that that was the right thing to do.

Robert Little

The purpose of making that statement was not to go against Malcolm—the purpose of making that statement was to fortify the Muslims. That's why I was brought to Chicago. When I got ready to make my statement, John Ali put a paper in front of me and told me I should read *that*. So I read the statement that was very negative for my mother. And it was negative against Malcolm. I wouldn't have read it over the air, you see, if I had looked at it. I asked John Ali about it and he says, "That's just a statement that was prepared for you to read." He said, "I know the Messenger will be very pleased with the way you read it," and that was it.

Abdul Aziz Omar

What stays in my mind is a picture that had Malcolm with horns on his head, and they were calling him a Judas. The cartoonists had made him with horns, and his head had been severed, and it was rolling down a hill or something. The language of ministers in the paper—I know Farrakhan was one of them, but there were other ministers, too—I read their language and said to myself, "They're trying to get him killed. They want him dead."

Imam Wallace D. Mohammed

I talked to Malcolm about the need to go someplace to sort of neutral territory and get out from everyone's influence and think through for myself leaving the Nation of Islam. And he said, "I think that's a very good idea. Where are you going?" And I said Minister Louis invited me to stay at his house in Boston. Malcolm laughed and he said, "That's not exactly what I'd call neutral territory." When I called Louis back to say I'd decided not to go to Boston, he really berated me. He said you didn't arrive at that conclusion yourself. You've been talking to somebody who's influenced you, and that person, whoever it is, is the devil, is somebody evil. Louis had clearly taken a very different kind of position of attempting to influence me, although he appeared to talk against that.

Amina Rahman

New York, 1964.

Malcolm X with Prince Al-Faysal, Saudi Arabia, April 1964.

Psychologically, I don't think Malcolm X ever made a complete break with the Nation of Islam. I think the Nation made a break with him. But in his mind, and in his planning, he never made a break with it.

John Henrik Clarke

Wherever Malcolm went in the Muslim world, he was accepted as a Muslim leader from the United States. He was accorded the status of a state leader, and as such we really saw in him somebody who represented the aspirations of the Africans, of the Asians, and of the Muslims, not only in the United States but in the whole of the western world. He was really considered the champion of freedom for the Afro-Asian countries.

Osman Ahmed

This is a postcard from Arabia: "Greetings from the ancient land of Arabia. Allah has blessed me to visit the Holy City of Mecca, where I witnessed pilgrims of all colors"—and "all colors" is underlined—"from all parts of this earth displaying a spirit of unity and brotherhood like I've never seen before. It is truly a sight to behold. El-Hajj Malik El-Shabazz." And I guess he thought I wouldn't know who that was, so in parentheses, he has "Malcolm X."

Gloria Richardson

I thought the Hajj would tie him down. Give him a walking stick so he could guide more carefully. Wake him up. Talk to him. Seek him out and bring him out of the field and put him in a role and let him hold his own.

Ella Collins

He saw that what he was advocating is not Islam. To me, that was the biggest impact.

Prince Mohmaed Al-Faysal

Cairo, August 1964.

Malcolm surrounded by African American friends: (*left to right*) Maya Angelou, Frank Robertson, Alice Windom, Accra, May 1964.

Opposite page: Malcolm with Mrs. Shirley Graham Du Bois, Accra, May 1964.

Malcolm's letter about his visit to Mecca is continuously misinterpreted. I talked to him soon after he arrived back in the U.S. He understood that the condition in the U.S. had not changed one iota.

John Henrik Clarke

Africans from all over the continent were to be found in Ghana, African Americans, West Indians. We learned to feel that here upon this rock we can build a nation, a Pan-Africanist nation.

Maya Angelou

It was heady, intoxicating, and into this boiling brew came Malcolm. Well, he was the man for the time. He was as large as the time. He wove such magic, and he dressed all of us in this rich fabric of his intelligence and insight.

Maya Angelou

Malcolm in front of Parliament House, Accra, May 1964. The statue of President Kwame Nkrumah was toppled during the 1966 coup.

When Malcolm addressed the students at the Great Hall at Legon, it was an electrifying experience. The hall was full. There was a sprinkling of whites, who had come, really—based on the comments they made before he started—to jeer and ridicule, and just to have an evening of entertainment. That mood changed as soon as Malcolm started to speak. Because of his consummate skill as an orator, it didn't matter what the nationality of his audience was.

Alice Windom

Malcolm X saw no contradiction between the African fight and the Black American fight in the United States, and he was not willing to sacrifice one for the other, inasmuch as he thought they were related. This would present a problem to some, because we had been estranged so long that in most cases we'd lost our political and spiritual connection to Africa.

John Henrik Clarke

Malcolm was invited for a luncheon by the Nigerian High Commissioner to Ghana, Alhaji Isa Wali, who had lived in the United States around African-American people. He wanted to receive Malcolm as a Muslim. He presented him with a beautiful blue robe, an orange turban, and a two-volume set of the holy Koran. He wanted to drape Malcolm's turban for him, and Malcolm, being six feet four, had to bend over at the waist while this turban was draped on him.

Alice Windom

Betty Shabazz shows (*left to right*) Ilyasah, Qubilah, and Attallah a map of Africa, while Malcolm travels there, 1964.

When my father was abroad, we had a world map on the living room wall, and anytime you got a little lonesome and wondered where Daddy was, we'd run over to that map. Where is he now? He's in Cairo, he's over here with Nkrumah. When he came back, we were connecting the dots, you know.

Attallah Shabazz

Malcolm wears a turban and robe and carries the Koran given to him by Alhaji Isa Wali, Nigerian High Commissioner to Ghana (*right*), Accra, May 1964.

Malcolm returns from abroad with a new Muslim name, El-Hajj Malik El-Shabazz, and with one bestowed on him in Nigeria, Alhadji Omowale (in Yoruba, "the child has come home"), New York, May 21, 1964.

Malcolm at founding rally of the Organization of African Unity,
Audubon Ballroom, Harlem, June 28, 1964.

On the morning of Malcolm's departure, Julian Mayfield, Maya Angelou, and a group of us went over to the Ambassador Hotel to take Malcolm to the airport. As we stood outside, chatting and taking pictures, Muhammad Ali and his brother came to the hotel from their morning walk. Malcolm had already told us it would be awkward for Muhammad Ali to be in his presence, because of the break with the Nation of Islam. So when we saw them coming, we didn't know what was going to happen. Muhammad Ali talked with most of us and was very courteous, but he did not speak to Malcolm.

Alice Windom

What was most wonderful about my father's returns from abroad is he looked different. He looked brand new—not just physical changes like a beard. I recall my sister, who was a baby when he first went away, trying to look past that beard and mustache to see if it was the same man. The more he traveled, the freer he became, the freer we became.

Attallah Shabazz

The *New York Post*, June 26, 1964, reports on an open letter to Elijah Muhammad, in which Malcolm X calls for an end to hostilities between their two groups.

Malcolm X to Elijah: Let's End the Fighting

Malcolm X today called for an end to the three-month dispute which has split the Black Muslim movement in Harlem.

In an open letter to Elijah Muhammad he urged an end to the hostilities which threaten to flare into open warfare between the two groups—his dissidents and the parent body headed by Elijah. He called for unity in solving the problems of egroes in Mississippi, Alabama, Georgia and other parts of the South.

"Instead of wasting all this energy fighting each other," he wrote, "we should be working in unity with other leaders and organizations in an effort to solve the very serious problems facing all Afro-Americans."

Poses a Question

He asked Elijah Muhammad how, since the Muslims did not resort to violence when they were attacked by "white racists" in Los Angeles, and Rochester, N. Y., they could justify declaring war on each other.

Malcolm X's statement came on the heels of an announcement by Muhammad's followers that they had received a "tip" from one of Malcolm's followers that plans were being made to assassinate Elijah Muhammad when he arrives at Kennedy Airport Sunday morning.

Fails to Show Up

The dramatic announcement of the "tip" came during a press conference at the Shabazz restaurant, a Muslim cafeteria at Lenox Av. and 116th St. Muhammad was to have announced plans to launch "his first economic program for Black America."

Muhammad did not appear. Instead, Minister James X, who described himself as Muhammad's "representative at this time and this place," read a prepared statement dealing with a forthcoming address by Elijah Muhammad on "economic independence for Black America."

Malcolm X, reached at his Boston hotel, denied that he or his followers were plotting to kill the Muslim leader. "I'm surprised at the accusation," he said. "No Muslim would think of assassinating Muhammad. He has never been in any danger in his life.

"We don't have to kill him. What he has done will bring him to his grave."

Muhammad's followers said that they would take every precaution to protect their leader. "We have our own security guards," they said. "We just want the police to know about the threat. Malcolm wants to regain his position by killing the Messenger."

Don't Think He'll Come'

Malcolm X scoffed at the accusation and said that the assassination threat was an excuse by Muhammad to bypass the June 28th speaking engagement. "I just don't think he'll come," he said.

The leader of the dissident Muslim group acknowledged that his followers were arming themselves but that the weapons were not for use against Negroes or Muslims. "All Negroes should own a rifle and use them to protect themselves with if the government can't do it."

When the OAAU was organized, and I was invited to go to an initial meeting, I had no idea what I was going to. I had just been told that this new nationalist organization was being formed. When I got there, we were all, about eight or ten people, sitting around talking. After about twenty minutes or so, Brother Malcolm came in with about three or four brothers. And I remember saying to myself, *Uh oh. You know, this is going to be serious.*

Peter Bailey

I was assigned by the New York City Police Department to infiltrate Malcolm's organization, report back membership, names, weapons, if any. And I attended meetings and was part of the security on occasions.

Gene Roberts

When Malcolm came back from Africa, the tensions between the two groups were still there. One, as far as I know, at that time Elijah Muhammad hadn't made a Hajj. The other was that Malcolm was getting nationwide publicity and worldwide support, and he had met with people who wouldn't sit down and talk to Elijah, meaning the heads of African states. There was an underlying feeling that he was getting too big for his pants, so to speak.

Gene Roberts

What the Nation lost during those years was not an immediate loss of membership, but a loss of future membership over the years that I don't think the Nation ever captured. There were people who simply never went in that direction because Malcolm wasn't there.

Amina Rahman

The impact of Malcolm leaving, or being sent away from the Nation of Islam, it meant we started growing more. The place would continue to be filled. In fact, we added on more.

Yusuf Shah

We was over at the restaurant; next thing we knew, Malcolm's followers come over there with guns. I mean, this was really a shock to us. We never carried any guns. And if they were carrying some, we didn't know anything about it. And then these things about Mr. Muhammad began to spread. True or false, they were spreading. And Malcolm's followers were the aggressors. If anybody is the aggressor, you have to defend yourself.

Yusuf Shah

Malcolm was supposed to meet some Muslims at his sister's house in Boston. I was told to go in Malcolm's place. After the meeting, we had just left in an old Cadillac, with a shotgun that we laid on the floor in the back of the car, because there was a Lincoln that was waiting for us. We knew they were Muslims from Farrakhan's mosque in Boston, so we were trying to get to the airport before they could catch up with us. But in the Callahan Tunnel they did catch up with us and blocked our car. They got out, and Goldberg raised the shotgun just for them to see it, but I tried to get the gun from him. I was going to fire. But they moved back to their car. We finally broke away and went into the airport, where police came up and arrested us.

Benjamin Karim

Malcolm relaxes with a delegation of Japanese peace activists at the home of Yuri Kochiyama, Harlem, June 4, 1964.

186

The Hiroshima Nagasaki World Peace Study Mission was coming through New York on its way to Europe and Moscow. There were three journalists with that group, and they wanted to meet Malcolm more than any other person in America. But it was only three months after Malcolm bolted from the Nation, and there were so many rumors that he would be killed before the end of May. People said, "Why would he take a chance and go to a stranger's place when his life was in danger?" But he did show, and I tell you, the place was jam packed. They were just so surprised at his graciousness, his warmth. And that he spoke about what he learned from reading when he was in prison — Chinese history, Japanese, Asian history in general. People were just lifting their eyebrows, Wow, all right!

Yuri Kochiyama

When the debates began at the UN around going into the Congo, several African diplomats, for the first time that I can remember, stood up, made speeches in which they tied events that were happening in the Congo to what was happening in Mississippi — this was the summer of 1964. This was revolutionary. The diplomats had not made that direct connection before — they would talk in oblique terms. I strongly believe that that's when the U.S. government realized, we gotta watch this man Malcolm X.

Peter Bailey

The three civil rights workers, James Chaney, Andrew Goodman, and Michael Schwerner, who disappeared in Philadelphia, Mississippi, in June, are pictured on a circular distributed by the FBI, 1964.

Egypt, August 1964.

Malcolm sent us twelve postcards from eleven different countries. From Egypt he said: "Greetings from the ancient valley of the Kings here in Luxor. After seven weeks amid the archeological sights of the ancient Nile, I feel like an expert in Egyptology, but I haven't forgotten our own problems there in the States even for one minute nor neglected it. Brother Malcolm."

Yuri Kochiyama

Harlem, July 1964. *Above*: Harlemites chant "we want justice" and carry "wanted for murder" posters with a photo of the police officer who shot fifteen-year-old James Powell to death. *Left:* A handbill passed out at 125th Street and Seventh Avenue during the rebellion.

During our riots in 1964, I remember people saying, "If Malcolm was here, he would do this or that." I had gotten a local radio station to permit us to be on the air. I made a telephone call to Minister Malcolm, who was abroad, and asked, "What advice would you give, Mr. Minister?" "Well, I'll tell you, counselor, I don't suggest you go stand on any car. Because if I was there, I would not."

Percy Sutton

He was the most wanted speaker on the college campuses, not only in the United States, but even abroad. He was invited to speak at the American University in Beirut. His lecture was attended by a massive number of students and Lebanese people.

Osman Ahmed

Atlantic City, August 1964. Supporters of the Mississippi Freedom Democratic Party (MFDP) at the Democratic National Convention. The historic challenge led by Fannie Lou Hamer of the MFDP to the all-white Mississippi delegation almost paralyzed activity at the convention.

Harlem, Williams Institutional C.M.E. Church, December 20, 1964. Malcolm, on stage with Mrs. Hamer and William Strickland of the Committee in Support of the MFDP Challenge.

Alex Haley and Malcolm work on the
autobiography, New York, 1963.

Malcolm was desperate at that time, so desperate it wasn't a choice between saying something and risking my life or keeping my mouth shut and keeping life. It was, I'm going to lose my life as it is, and I'm going to do what I can to let the truth be known before I'm killed.

Imam Wallace D. Mohammed

Malcolm had a Liberation School, but he was busy traveling all the time; James Campbell actually ran the school. The children's classes had a lot of geography about Africa, and for the adults it was much more political and would combine African and African-American history. One thing Malcolm said was, "A school is not four walls and a roof. It is whenever you can get one person willing to teach and one who's willing to learn." And he said that all of us should play both sides—"Sometimes we are teachers, and sometimes we are students."

Yuri Kochiyama

Cairo, August 1964. Malcolm X attends the Organization of African Unity conference and remains in Egypt for two months. *Right:* He meets with Sheik Abdel Rahman Tag (*right*), future rector of Al Azhar, the only Muslim university in the world; *below right*: discusses the Koran at the Semiramis Hotel; and *opposite*: converses with Egyptian man.

The letter that Minister Malcolm wrote from Mecca in the fall for release to the press concerning Muslims who showed no signs of racism — it took a lot of gall for him to do that. But, see, one thing about Minister Malcolm, he would always tell the truth, regardless of what anyone thought of it. When he wrote this letter back, I was afraid of how the people in the Nation of Islam would try to use it against him — which they did.

Benjamin Karim

193

During a meeting in a little coffee shop at the hotel there in Nairobi, Malcolm would say, "Always sit with your back to the wall, so you can look out and see who is watching you." I had a feeling from our discussions that Malcolm was in the process of becoming a changed man. He kept saying over and over that he really wanted to be helpful and supportive of the civil rights movement. And he wanted to visit the South.

John Lewis

The last time I saw Malcolm, in October '64 in Ethiopia—I was living there by that time—Malcolm was there trying to see Emperor Haile Selassie. He met with no success, because the Ethiopian government was dependent on the U.S. There were governments that weren't about to exercise any manhood that would make them do something that the American government didn't want.

Alice Windom

Student Nonviolent Coordinating Committee (SNCC) members demonstrate, 1960s.

New York, Kennedy Airport, November 24, 1964. Malcolm returns home to Betty and the children and also to a family reunion with his mother and siblings in Lansing.

I'd tell Malcolm, you know, none of us is ever going to amount to anything until we get our mother out of Kalamazoo. It had preyed on my mind for years. The next thing I knew I got a call, my mother was in Lansing at my brother Philbert's. And we went to see her. It was a joyous time.

Yvonne Woodward

The hurtful thing to me was that Malcolm never really had the time and the opportunity to get to know our mother as she was at that point. She was a very strong woman. A very proud woman. And she had withstood a great deal of pressure and anguish and "treatment" in the mental health system.

Robert Little

When Maya Angelou came back to the States, she wanted to work with Malcolm. She was ready to help him develop this organization. Those of us who were going to stay in Africa wanted to build a significant branch in Africa that would cover all the countries we were living in; we were in several countries by the end of 1964.

Alice Windom

The effort to bring the condition of not just Black America and Africa, but the situation of colonialism, before the United Nations—I thought it was an excellent strategy. It was a master stroke on his part, well thought out, well documented, and very forcefully delivered. It was practiced on the street corners of New York, and at every gathering he would mention it.

Percy Sutton

Harlem, Audubon Ballroom, December 13, 1964. Malcolm greets guest speakers at an OAAU meeting, Sudanese Sheik Ahmed Hassoun from Mecca (in turban) and Abu Mohammed Babu, radical government minister from Tanzania, whom Malcolm met in Tanzania.

You'd see statements in the Muslim paper itself. There were articles being written by Farrakhan suggesting that Malcolm should be dead. There were statements being made all over the country in the various FOI classes, and the national authorities would come around and say things. When Malcolm came back from Africa, I'd tell him to just hush and forget about this whole thing and go to Africa and stay over there and let this thing cool down.

Wilfred Little

Muhammad Speaks runs a five-page denunciation of Malcolm X by Minister Louis X (now Farrakhan) of Boston, December 4, 1964. "Such a man as Malcolm is worthy of death," he writes.

Boston Minister Tells of Malcolm—Muhammad's Biggest Hypocrite

Saved—By Messenger's Guidance

By Minister Louis X
(Boston, Mass.)

It is hinted, according to the *New York Times* newspaper (Sunday, Nov. 8, 1964; pg. 48, column one) that Malcolm is returning to the States. We, therefore, would like to ask the questions:

IS Malcolm bold enough to return and face the music—since he

Minister Louis

ordered the notes to be played — after bowing

EDITOR'S NOTE: Thousands of shocked black Americans have become deeply resentful of the shameful attempts by defector and hypocrite Malcolm to slander and destroy the great Islamic leader, the Honorable Elijah Muhammad, who lifted him from obscurity and placed him in a position of national prominence and trust. The vicious slanders of this particular defector, while doomed to failure, have caused concern not only among the ranks of Muslims, but among many fair-minded non-Muslims.

The divinely-guided mission of Mr. Muhammad, however, has exposed the envy, jealousy and emptiness of this defector, which has disgraced not only himself but all those who have associated with him.

The following objective article from Minister Louis of Boston is printed in response to demands for a definitive statement on the acts of this particular character, who has resorted to becoming an international hobo, without home or followers. It is a lesson on how a slanderer

GAINING HIS guidance directly from the Messenger of Allah, (center) rather than from defectors world heavyweight champion, Muhammad Ali (r.) and his brother, Rahaman Ali (l.) have moved steadily towards success in their fields, with the respect of admirers around the world in sharp contrast to attempts by once-Minister Malcolm to defame and destroy his former teacher. Here the champion and his brother take a lesson from the Holy Qur-an from Mr. Muhammad.

Malcolm, under police guard, with Gene Roberts, leaves a radio station after a report that an attempt was to be made on his life. Four of Malcolm's followers were assaulted by members of the Nation of Islam temple, Philadelphia, late December 1964.

What I was seeing was a man who was valiant beyond belief, whose structural world was tottering, and he was trying to hold it together. What he needed, and what he wanted, and what he was trying to do was somehow to maintain a public presence until he could build up his own organization.

Alex Haley

Malcolm couldn't stop speaking to the media, because he would be sacrificing his audience. When he was holding meetings in Harlem, typically no more than a thousand people would attend. More often, four, five hundred. He had in mind a national and, indeed, a global audience, and his only access to that audience was the mass media, and television, especially.

Peter Goldman

Sister Betty was pregnant again. And that was about the only joyous thing happening to Malcolm at that time. Around him otherwise were organizations, agencies, vying for him to join them. The moderates, the church groups wanted Malcolm to be an an example of conversion, so to speak. And the other groups wanted him because of the very potency of his name.

Alex Haley

Betty Shabazz and the children, 1964.

199

Malcolm had come to Tuskegee Institute during the Selma demonstrations. We went up there and asked Malcolm if he would come and speak to some of the Selma youngsters. We had taken youngsters from Mississippi up to Harlem in December '64, and Malcolm had talked to them about the world struggle and how Black people in Mississippi and Harlem fit into it.

Cleveland Sellers

Doug and Tina Harris, who were on SNCC's staff at that time, would get Malcolm's speech from the Audubon taped and sent down every week from their contacts in New York to the Selma SNCC office. Copies would be passed around among the staff people. Bob Mants and myself, working outside of Selma in Lowndes County, would play Malcolm X throughout the week inside of Lowndes County.

Stokely Carmichael

Above: Malcolm addressed several thousand students at Tuskegee Institute, Alabama, February 3, 1965, and, *bottom*, voting rights activists, Brown Chapel A.M.E. Church, Selma, Alabama, the next day.

Paris, November 1964. Malcolm is interviewed by a Black reporter. On his way home from Africa, Malcolm had spoken to an overflow crowd at a program sponsored by the African cultural organization, Presence Africaine. He was barred from entering France on a return trip, February 9, 1965.

I don't think Elijah Muhammad could've caused Charles de Gaulle to up and say don't let Malcolm X into France. I have a feeling that the French government was reacting to a request from the United States. The OAAU Paris was organizing the Africans, and the French didn't want these people organized. So they would've been very open to a request of that type from the United States.

Peter Bailey

In the rear of the car sat Malcolm with two people, one on each side, as was the habit when we left court. I said to him, "Doesn't this disturb you having these people with guns?" He said, "No, but it makes them happy." And he says, "Have I told you the story of Omar the slave? Omar said to his master, 'Give me your fastest horse, I'm going to escape the Face of Death,' it being a slave belief that if you rode by day and got through the day with the swiftness of the horse, you were safe by night. There were seven paths down which Omar could go. He started down the center path, pulled the horse back. Started to the left, and pulled back again. Only a short distance down the third path stood the Face of Death. Death said to Omar, 'For three days I've waited at this spot for you to come. Why has it taken you so long?'" And then Minister Malcolm said, "So you see, counselor, you can twist, you can turn, but there's a destiny, so it really doesn't bother me having them here."

Percy Sutton

Malcolm leaves his firebombed house, East
Elmhurst, Queens, February 14, 1965.

Part of the audience at an OAAU program, Audubon
Ballroom, Harlem, February 15, 1965.

I remember Malcolm literally crying out one night. He said, "I'm trying to turn the corner, but they won't let me." One night Malcolm's home was bombed, and I remember feeling sometimes as if I wanted to hug him, just go up and hug your brother or something because he was under such pressure, and yet his discipline, his image demanded that he be stoic and move on.

Alex Haley

When Malcolm's house was fire-bombed, there were a lot of rumors. The police department did it, the FBI-CIA did it, Elijah's people. But everybody agreed to the fact that he was in mortal danger.

Gene Roberts

The meeting that Malcolm had was on the Monday following the house bombing. I was standing up front along with about four or five other guys, and I heard commotion in the middle to my right. I see this young fella come down the middle aisle and slip into about the second or third row and take a seat. He was wearing a blue suit, white shirt and a red bow tie, which is basically the uniform for the Nation of Islam. I remember seeing a couple of people there that I hadn't seen before at the meetings, and I mentioned their names. After the meeting I reported back to the department that I felt I had just seen a dry run on Malcolm's life. And they said, "We'll take care of it." And that was that.

Gene Roberts

A pregnant Betty and the four girls at Malcolm's side, OAAU office, Harlem, mid-February 1965.

I felt as though something very heavy was pressing down on my shoulders, as though I was weighing twice as much as my normal weight. In other words, I could feel my weight at the point that my feet touched the floor. I felt that there was something ominous in the air. When you work very closely with a person, their feelings can be transferred, so to speak. You may not be able to read it directly and tell what it's all about, but you can pick up these vibrations.

Benjamin Karim

It wasn't something special, it was out of the ordinary. When my mother received the call from my father for us to all get together and come down to the Audubon, I knew that was different. That was a rhythm change with all of the things that were going on. And all the while it was still an exciting adventure to get ready and go see Daddy, 'cause we were living in a house with another family.

Attallah Shabazz

1964.

I went back and Minister Malcolm asked, "How are you going to open up?" I told him I would open up in such a way that the audience would accept the fact that he did not have the OAAU charter again, after promising so many times. He said okay, and I went on stage. Malcolm had a way of walking across the floor. Unless you were looking, you didn't even know. He had set down behind me, and he placed a sheet of paper on a chair. When I looked down at my notes, I saw his hand reach for the paper. Evidently, he recognized that I had seen his hand reach for that piece of paper, and he said, "Make it plain." *Make it plain* is the code word that he used for us to bring him forward. He didn't like a lot of icing and all that. Just, just plain.

Benjamin Karim

The whole place was in an uproar. I wanted to get up there and be near Malcolm, so I followed this young brother. He might have been security for Malcolm, because what he did was go right behind the curtains to see if anybody was behind there. I went to Malcolm's body, and I put his head on my lap. Then a short time later someone tapped me and said, Can you help at the side? The youngest baby needed bottle feeding at the time, and so I went to the side room and fed the baby.

Yuri Kochiyama

204

I remember Betty attempting to give him artificial respiration. She was just pumping his arms, and I could see it was futile. Then she just said, "Oh, no, he's gone, and I'm pregnant." I just, oh, I never felt so bad. I remember Attallah's face, red, blood red, crying and screaming down there in the seats where she's sitting.

Muriel Feelings

It's amazing how protective you are of your parents without them even knowing it. It meant more to me to comfort my mother, to at least hope that she was all right. After he was indeed shot, we were moved back behind the stage, and my mother went onto the stage with her husband. A lot of mayhem and confusion took place. I felt old from that point on.

Attallah Shabazz

A man came to give mouth-to-mouth resuscitation. At that time I was in the side room, so I probably didn't see him, but when the papers came out with the picture of Gene Roberts, I couldn't believe it.

Yuri Kochiyama

Harlem, February 21, 1965. Gene Roberts (*kneeling*) tries to resuscitate Malcolm X on the stage of the Audubon Ballroom.

At that time, I knew that he was dead. He was dead. And that's when I happened to look around, and I saw my wife standing in the back, off into the wings. So I saw that she was okay, I got her out and got her a cab and sent her home. I remember her giving me a bullet shell. A nine millimeter, I believe it was. And I sent her home.

Gene Roberts

February 21, 1965. Outside the Audubon Ballroom, policemen struggle with assassin Talmadge Hayer (a.k.a. Thomas Hagan), on floor, while protecting him from crowd. Hayer is carried away by police.

When I heard the chairs being thrown aside on the stage, I knew then that it was aimed at him. Then some brothers bust through and knocked the door open. And I saw him lying there on the stage, and I knew he was gone. I felt whatever the thing was that had set upon my shoulder like double gravity was gone. And I felt a relief for him, believe it or not.

Benjamin Karim

I was facing the assassins, so I saw them stand up and take my father's life. Through junior high school, I wondered if I could have prevented it. You know, that kind of feeling—not responsible, but could I have saved my father?

Attallah Shabazz

February 21, 1965. Malcolm's supporters and police wheel Malcolm across the street to the Columbia Presbyterian Hospital.

I just remember, too, how long it took the ambulance to get there, and the hospital was just across the street from the Audubon. I heard other stories, about people who saw one of the assassins jump into a police car. I went with Betty across the street to the hospital. When I got there, they had just pronounced him dead. I saw Betty's position being such a—it was just a nightmare.

Muriel Feelings

There was a squad car that I noticed on the corner out front. I don't remember seeing too many others, with the exception of being across the street at the hospital. Why it was set up that way, I have no idea. But that also seemed odd, coming on the aftermath of his house being bombed and everything else.

Gene Roberts

A newsman points to bullet holes in the podium, Audubon Ballroom, February 21, 1965.

We were watching excerpts from the news flashes on Malcolm. Betty would look at them for a while, as long as she could, and then cover her eyes and turn and look at the wall. And then she'd go toward the kitchen, for no reason whatsoever. One of the little girls put her hand in Betty's and says, "Mama, is Daddy comin' home?" She says, "No, honey, Daddy's not coming home." You know, just like that.

Gordon Parks

Betty Shabazz leaves the city morgue with Percy Sutton (*left*) and funeral director Joseph Hall, February 22, 1965.

I was going to the Audubon that day. Had been out the night before, reading. Had gotten lazy and had said simply, I'll go next week. And so proceeded to go into the kitchen, put some coffee on, turn on the radio. A flash came through on this station and said Malcolm had been assassinated. And I froze. I remember turning in that kitchen and screaming. I remember walking down to my bedroom to put my clothes on. And I remember cursing myself for not being there.

Sonia Sanchez

I wasn't remorseful. I'm telling you the truth. I was there taking the brunt of what his people, who said they were with him, were doing. And nobody else around knows like I know. I was there. They're guessing, but I know. And so therefore, I wasn't remorseful, I wasn't sorry. For what? And as Mr. Muhammad said, "He talked violence, and he died violent." And he was a hypocrite. And I say that he was a Benedict Arnold.

Yusuf Shah

The Honorable Elijah Muhammad said, "I wish that hadn't been done." He was talking about the assassination of Malcolm. That's all I heard from his mouth at that time. But I will tell you that I know from reliable sources that when Malcolm was really causing serious trouble for the Honorable Elijah Muhammad, the Honorable Elijah Muhammad expressed deep hurt and anger before the staff.

Imam Wallace D. Mohammed

Boston, February 25, 1965. Ella Collins, Malcolm's half sister, tells newspeople she intends "to carry out, as far as possible, all the objectives of my brother."

Mourners outside Unity Funeral Home, Harlem, February 25, 1965. Malcolm's body was viewed by 22,000 people between February 23 and 26.

I think Malcolm X was killed by a combination of the Nation of Islam manipulated by more skillful forces and more powerful forces. I do not think the Nation of Islam had the men who would plan something as big as that. It was planned with skill, and I think it had been planned for a number of Sundays, but was brought off the first Sunday there was no search at the door. So the planners were in place.

John Henrik Clarke

Malcolm was assassinated in a very public way so that hands seen pulling the trigger were Black. That put that thing into it. I think it was also designed to intimidate his supporters. You know, we can shoot your leader down in the middle of the afternoon, and there's nothing you can do about it.

Peter Bailey

Nation of Islam Mosque No. 7 is gutted in an early morning fire, Harlem, February 23, 1965.

I guess you could say the mood was like that moonlit night when Manhattan went into darkness. Then someone blew up the old mosque, evidently with thoughts of provoking violence between the Muslims who were with Malcolm and Muslims who were still in the Nation of Islam. But that didn't work because we both knew we wouldn't burn the mosque. I mean, you could find very few Black people that would set their churches on fire.

Benjamin Karim

Chicago Coliseum, February 26, 1965. Wilfred X, minister of Mosque No. 1 in Detroit, addresses the Nation of Islam Savior's Day convention.

At Savior's Day, the Honorable Elijah Muhammad was there, and they asked my brother Wilfred to speak and they asked me to speak. I don't remember verbatim, but I did say that no man likes to hear that his brother is dead— no man. My brother made some statements to that same effect. And then that was it. It was over.

Abdul Aziz Omar

Elijah Muhammad, walled in by Fruit of Islam guards, tells the Savior's Day crowd that Malcolm was "a hypocrite" who "got what he was preaching."

He was indeed our manhood. You know, our shining Black prince who didn't hesitate to die because he loved us so. I thought that in honoring him we honored the best in ourselves, and I wanted that to be a part of what the world would remember when they thought of Malcolm.

Ossie Davis

Malcolm's body, wrapped in traditional white sheets for Muslim funeral and burial, Faith Temple Church of God in Christ, Harlem, February 27, 1965.

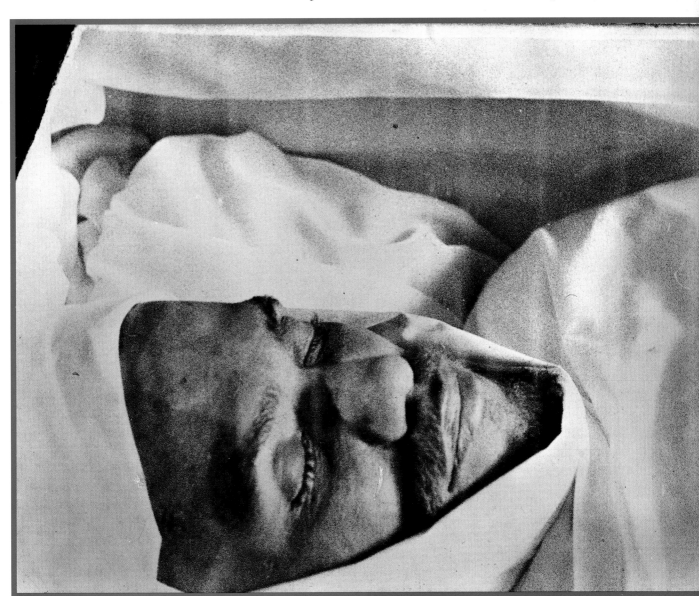

Malcolm's funeral. Betty Shabazz in veil at
casket, February 27, 1965.

There were five of us, and I wanted desperately to go, and the others said no, because there were so many threats. We watched it from a television in our hotel room. Then we had to leave to get back to Michigan, and it was a sad, sad thousands of miles for me.

Yvonne Woodward

In Islam, we consider Malcolm as a martyr: a person who died fighting for a cause, for an Islamic cause, for the brotherhood of all human beings, and that we lost a dear brother.

Osman Ahmed

Sheik Ahmed Hassan Jaaber prays over the
closed casket, February 27, 1965.

February 27, 1965. Pallbearers carry Malcolm's casket.

Those of us in the Student Nonviolent Coordinating Committee that represented people in the front line in the South, we felt that we had to be there. There was no other place to be, but to be there, to bear witness to the life and times of Malcolm.

John Lewis

We felt like we were bringing a message to Malcolm. And that message was, we heard you, we were listening. We have taken the best of what you offered, and we will continue to incorporate that movement in our struggle.

Cleveland Sellers

215

A woman reaches out to bid farewell to Malcolm.

Covering Malcolm's casket, Ferncliff
Cemetery, Hartsdale, New York,
February 27, 1965.

When we got to the cemetery, the professional grave diggers were standing there with their shovels, but some of the Black brothers said, no, uh uh. We dig this grave. We cover this brother with dirt. And it was a moving moment, and I was proud at that moment to be Black. And proud that my community and people, no matter what had been said by the outside world, said to the brother, we loved and respected and admired you. And so we buried him, and there it is.

Ossie Davis

After funeral service, last mourners kneel to the East in final prayer at Malcolm's grave, Ferncliff Cemetery, Hartsdale, New York, February 27, 1965.

He was lying in state in a Harlem mortuary. I just got in line and went filing along with the other people. And there he was in the casket. I said to myself, but to him just barely audibly, "Bye, Red," 'cause he liked to be called Red by those who knew him very well. I never had called him Red to his face, but I felt now I was among those close to him, and so I just said "Bye, Red" and filed on past.

Alex Haley

THE
MAN WHO
ALMOST CHANGED
AMERICA

The *Autobiography of Malcolm X* had gone through thirty-three printings and Malcolm himself had been dead for twenty-seven years, when in 1992, Spike Lee's galactically promoted film on the life of Malcolm X opened in America. The film's eagerly anticipated release marked the crest of a virtual Malcolmania, which had swept over America since the late

Opposite page: Partial view of exterior wall mural produced by
Save the Audubon Coalition activists,
Audubon Ballroom, Harlem, 1992.

eighties. Turned on by the racial references of rappers like Public Enemy and KRS-1, turned off by the dismissive racism of the Reagan-Bush era and the largely irrelevant responses of traditional "race leaders" to the crises of their lives, young Black America embraced Malcolm as the symbol of indomitable Blackness they found so lacking in modern times.

From young Blacks, the phenomenon spread to "hip" young whites—and Malcolm was "in." The "free market" then joined the hype, turning what had been new consciousness for some into new commercial opportunities for others. Soon America was flooded with Malcolm records and Malcolm calendars, Malcolm caps and Malcolm raps (on new CDs). There were Malcolm T-shirts and Malcolm sweatshirts; Malcolm jumpsuits and Malcolm jewelry; Malcolm handicrafts and Malcolm statuary; Malcolm posters and—I am told—Malcolm potato chips packaged in racially correct red, black, and green. The *Autobiography* was in every airport bookstore, and every newspaper, seemingly, had a retrospective article on Malcolm.

Not to be outdone, magazines from *Rolling Stone* on the left to *National Review* on the right featured articles on Malcolm or on what many saw as the same thing—Spike's anxiously awaited film.

Malcolm was hot, so the votaries flocked to the rekindled funeral altar to light a candle and, perhaps, make a buck or two. From all over the political spectrum they came to interpret, and reinterpret, the "Meaning of Malcolm X."

The conservatives, for example, claimed Malcolm as an apostle of "limited government" and "self-help" because he had said: "Black people had to build within themselves much greater awareness that along with equal rights there had to be the bearing of equal responsibilities."

The integrationists claimed him because, after his trip to Mecca, he wrote back to his followers and to the American press: "In the past, yes, I have made sweeping indictments of *all* white people. I will never be guilty of that again—as I know now that some white people *are* truly sincere, that some truly are capable of being brotherly toward a Black man. The true Islam has shown me that a blanket indictment of all white people is as wrong as when whites make blanket indictments against Blacks."

The Marxists claimed Malcolm as a representative of the "revolutionary proletariat," because he had appeared at several forums sponsored by the Socialist Workers Party, and at one of them, asked what political and economic system he favored, had replied, "I don't know but I'm flexible. . . . All of the countries that are emerging today from under the shackles of colonialism are turning toward socialism. I don't think it's an accident. Most of the countries that were colonial powers were capitalist countries and the last bulwark of capitalism today is America. It's impossible for a white person to believe in capitalism and not believe in racism. You can't have capitalism without racism." The SWP didn't dwell overmuch on the fact that Malcolm's anticapitalism was linked indissolubly with his antiracism.

The Black nationalists, of course, viewed Malcolm as indisputably theirs, so they regarded all this opportunistic heresy with alarm and disdain . . . and then some of them printed up their own T-shirts.

In death, then, Malcolm's memory became a prize to be fought over. Some wanted to sharpen his image; others to blur it. Some wanted to "humanize" Malcolm, while others wanted to iconize him. Malcolm was made historically elastic, pulled to and fro by the tag teams of political correctness, mercantile hucksterism, and status-quo apologetics.

But I do not believe that we can discern Malcolm's real significance in the hullabaloo of recent years. Instead I think it can be found in the two decades or so that preceded the Elvis-like frenzy, when interest in Malcolm flowed beneath America like an unseen river.

Sometimes the river of Malcolm's legacy surfaced as a Birthday Memorial Committee or a school in Chicago, Illinois, or Greensboro, North Carolina. Sometimes it gushed forth on New York's West 166th Street, as the Save the Audubon Coalition, and sometimes it spilled out onto Harlem's 125th Street, as the Malcolm X Lovers Network of Afram Associates, Inc. At other times the river was a memorial foundation in Omaha or the baptismal waters for the countless children christened Malik or Malika, Malaika or Malcolm. Whatever and wherever, the river of Malcolm ran on, refreshing the banks of memory and roiling the waters of discovery.

Really to appreciate Malcolm, I think, is to appreciate the enduring power of this river, swollen by the incoming streams of new and old believers who have looked into the waters of Malcolm's life and seen reflected there a vision of change for themselves and for America.

That is why Malcolm's power to touch, move, instruct, awaken, inspire, convert, motivate, influence, and enlighten from beyond the grave has necessitated a counterresponse from those who still feel endangered by him, to make his legacy more accessible, less confrontational, less jagged, less—well—racial . . . more human, as it were. But the meaning of Malcolm does not lie in the often self-serving scrounging around in the minutiae of his life engaged in by some biographers, any more than the significance of George Washington lies in his wooden teeth and childless marriage or that of Abraham Lincoln's in his third-ballot nomination as the compromise candidate of the Republican party in the presidential election of 1860.

Rather, Washington's and Lincoln's significance, like Malcolm's, lies in their impact upon their times and in how they conducted themselves in the wars they led on behalf of their people's interests: in Malcolm's case, the leadership he provided in the Great Race War that convulsed America in the fifth and sixth decades of this century.

Malcolm's lasting contribution to the struggle of Black people—and to the possible rescue of America—is his analysis of the destructive power of American racism. Malcolm did not live long enough to change America himself, but his analysis of racism gave Black folks the cultural and intellectual keys to re-create ourselves and redefine America. His critique was vital, because it demystified white America and the white West, puncturing their historical claims, and wrenching loose their monopolistic hold on the idea and personhood of "humanity."

Before Malcolm, we knew we were not free, but we had an inferiority complex. We conked our hair, used bleaching creams on our skin, wore stocking caps to make our hair lie flat. But Malcolm asked us, "Who taught you to hate the color of your skin? Who taught you to hate the texture of your hair? Who taught you to hate the shape of your nose? Who taught you to hate yourself from the top of your head to the soles of your feet? Who taught you to hate your own kind? Who taught you to hate the race you belong to so much so that you don't want to be around each other?...You should ask yourself, 'Who taught you to hate being what God gave you?'" Those questions liberated our spirit and reincluded us in the family of humankind.

Malcolm then liberated our minds by ruthlessly dissecting America. On the police: "We live in a police state." On integration: "They don't want you. Why, as soon as you move in, they're there for a while, and then they're gone, and you're left there all by yourself." On the law: "It doesn't protect you, doesn't work for you and is not enforced." On white liberals: "They only want to control you." And on government: "We can see that it is nothing but a governmental conspiracy to continue to deprive the Black people in this country of their rights. And the only way we will get these rights restored is by taking it out of Uncle Sam's hands. Take him to court and charge him with genocide, the mass murder of millions of Black people in this country—political murder, economic murder, social murder, mental murder."

Those accusations are why America has called Malcolm a "hater." But that is vintage tricknology, as Malcolm used to phrase it. For, then and now, America has never said that what Malcolm said was untrue.

Malcolm's legacy, therefore, is that he discerned the hidden meaning behind America's racial posture, the private interests beneath the public words. Like Prometheus, Malcolm stole the flame of secret knowledge and set America on fire.

In Their Own Words

Osman Ahmed	Friend; met Malcolm X while a student at Dartmouth
Prince Mohmaed Al-Faysal	Crown Prince of Saudi Arabia
Maya Angelou	Writer, poet; friend and associate from Africa trips
John Henrik Clarke	Historian; member of OAAU
Muriel Feelings	Member of OAAU
Benjamin Karim	Close associate of Malcolm in the Nation of Islam and Muslim Mosque, Inc.
Yuri Kochiyama	Harlem community activist; associate of Malcolm X
Sonia Sanchez	Poet, writer
Yusuf Shah	Captain, Fruit of Islam, Mosque No. 7
Percy Sutton	Friend and attorney of Malcolm X
Alice Windom	Friend and associate of Malcolm X in Africa
Yvonne Woodward	Malcolm X's younger sister

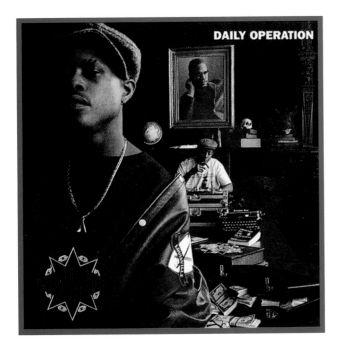

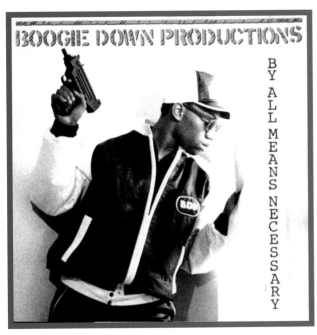

Rap stars use Malcolm X's image, voice, and ideas in their music and videos. Gangstarr CD *Daily Operation*, 1992. KRS-1, inspired by Malcolm X's famous pose, on Boogie Down Productions CD, *By All Means Necessary*, 1988.

What did Minister Malcolm leave? He left a beautiful woman of high intelligence who reared children and educated them with a dignity unlike that you normally see. He left a lot of people wearing X's on their skull caps and X's on their bicycle caps, without any understanding of what Malcolm X was, and he left other people who were well-grounded in who Malcolm X was. He left a sense of eloquence that one would want to mimic, he left a sense of strength that others want to follow, and he left, most of all, a quandary as to who was Malcolm X.

Percy Sutton

A Black Panther Party storefront headquarters, Harlem, early 1970s.

Teenager demonstrates against a meeting of the Ku Klux Klan and other hate groups, South Central Los Angeles, February 1, 1992.

I saw a man laying in there, but that wasn't Malcolm. In my mind, I didn't let him die. I used to wait 'til my family went up to the cottage for the weekend, and I would get out all his tapes. I had tapes of his speeches. And I would spend the weekend sewing and listening to Malcolm. I kept Malcolm alive for years.

Yvonne Woodward

New Orleans, March 1992.

I know often when people talk about Malcolm X, they make him seem larger than life, and that's dangerous. Because young people, hearing about him—this larger-than-life person—will be led to think they could never be like him, you see. He's not accessible, then. The truth is, the man was as large as life, a man of great profundity, with a wonderful sense of humor and a loving sense of his people.

Maya Angelou

His strength was his ability to select people that could help him. That was his strength. His weakness was that he had a criminal mind, and that he was intoxicated with the cameras and microphones. And that he could give out punishment, or he could give out reprimand, but he couldn't take it when his time come. And I will not back down off of that, because I'm speaking from knowledge.

Yusuf Shah

I see him as a man who hated ignorance with a passion. That's right. He was a fanatic about learning, about knowledge. And I see him as having an undying love for and a commitment to justice. He hated injustice. I think what he fought most for was justice. And he had an unwavering belief in God. But that aside, he was for justice.

Benjamin Karim

Man pickets white-owned liquor store in Black community, Chicago, late 1960s.

228

Man confronts police during period of racial unrest, Crown
Heights, Brooklyn, New York, August 20, 1991.

He had an extraordinarily quick mind. He was a genius. He also had this very high level of integrity. When they listen to the tapes of his speeches now, it's important that people remember: when he was speaking out and calling white people the names that he called them, we were still getting off the sidewalks for them to walk by in parts of this country.

Alice Windom

A girl views placards of Elijah Muhammad and Malcolm X at a demonstration against the U.S. role in the Persian Gulf War, Harlem, February 1991.

I think he was a great loss, and especially to America. Because here is a man who has, in spite of his starting as a racist, sectarian person, developed into a force of reconciliation. And had he been given a chance, Malcolm would have changed American society, more than anybody else in recent history.

Prince Mohmaed Al-Faysal

When he said things like, "If you don't know where your people have come from and who you are, how will you know what direction to go?"—for us Asians it gave us a clue to where we should begin.

Yuri Kochiyama

He said it in a very strong fashion, a very manly fashion, one that says, "I am not afraid to say what you've been thinking all these years." That's why we loved him so very much. He said it out loud. Not behind closed doors. He took on America for us.

Sonia Sanchez

Tattered poster on outside wall, Audubon Ballroom, Harlem, September 28, 1990.

Vendor display, West 125th Street, Harlem, 1989.

I think he is probably the one person in the latter half of this twentieth century who had more impact on the development of institutions—the bookstores and the independent school movement and the travel to Africa. The internationalization of our struggle—our awareness of the Caribbean and Africa—has come from his influence.

Muriel Feelings

A re-creation of Nation of Islam rally, in Spike Lee's *Malcolm X*, 1992.
Denzel Washington, as Malcolm, is at podium.

I've heard some people say, "We know what Malcolm would have said" about this or that situation today. To say that is to freeze him in time and in a set of opinions. That's completely antithetical to him. Malcolm's ideas were not canned—they were alive and evolving.

Amina Rahman

Betty Shabazz addresses Malcolm X conference before giant poster displaying his image, New York, 1992.

Malcolm could have had anything he wished. He could have had the position he wished. But he wasn't aspiring for any of that. He was in the line of the prophets.

Osman Ahmed

234

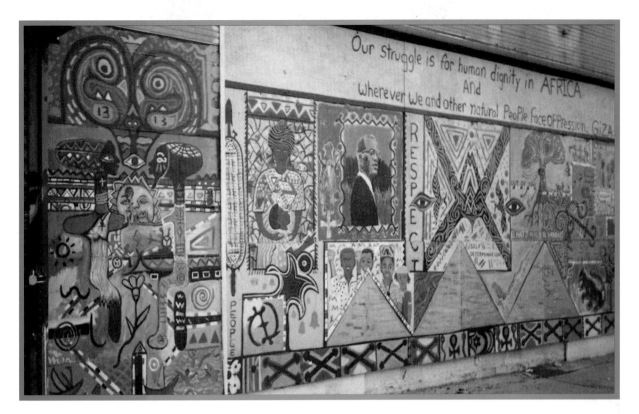

Section of exterior wall mural produced by Save the Audubon Coalition
activists, Audubon Ballroom, Harlem, 1992.

We have buried the body of Malcolm, we have not buried the spirit. We have not buried
the teachings. We have not buried the mission. We have not buried the legacy. So we've heard
him once, we will hear him again. Hearing is one thing, heeding him is another. I think if we
hear him and heed him, we will make a better world for our children and their children, and
the still more beautiful ones not yet born.

John Henrik Clarke

NOTES

THE HISTORY THAT MADE MALCOLM
(1925–1940)

p.   7   "WE ARE GOING TO HAVE DEMOCRACY": Vincent, *Garvey*, p. 117

p.   7   A SURVEILLANCE PROGRAM: O'Reilly, pp. 13–14

p.   8   "SOUTHERN EXTREMISTS PROCEEDED": Woodward, p. 353

p.   11   THE LITTLES SEEM TO HAVE BEEN SUCCESSFUL ENOUGH IN THEIR POLITICAL WORK: Vincent, *Black Scholar*, pp. 12–13

p.   13   "I COULDN'T HAVE FEIGNED INDIFFERENCE": Haley, p. 35

GROWING AND OUTGROWING THE NATION (1953–1963)

p.   71   "I CAN'T START TO DESCRIBE FOR YOU": Haley, p. 217

p.   72   "AN UNKNOWN NUMBER OF SMALLER MISSIONS": Essien-Udom, p. 343

p.   73   AND THERE WAS CESAR CHAVEZ: Acuna, p. 269

p.   73   "DISAGREED" WITH THE "SELF-DEFEATING WAITING VIEW": Haley, p. 198

p.   79   "NOT TO SAY ANY OF THAT ROMANCE STUFF": Haley, pp. 231–232

p.   80   THE TWO-FAMILY HOUSE IN QUEENS: Evanzz, p. 73

p.   80   "NO BLACK MAN, EVEN IN MISSISSIPPI": FBI, p. 440

p.   81   "DELIBERATELY RIPPED THEIR SUIT JACKETS": Evanzz, p. 118

p.   82   "THEY WAITED ON WORD": Friedly, p. 117

p.   83   "BROTHER MALCOLM, I WANT YOU TO BECOME WELL KNOWN": Haley, p. 268

p.   85   "WHILE CITY OFFICIALS": Carson, p. 160

p.   85   "THE TELEPHONE IN OUR SMALL TEMPLE": Haley, p. 242

p.   85   CONTRARY TO MIKE WALLACE'S HOPES: Lincoln, p. 112-113

p.   87   "WORKED AS SOME OF THEM DID FOR THE WHITE MAN": Haley, p. 267

FIGHTING ON THREE FRONTS
(1964–1965)

EPILOGUE:
THE MAN WHO ALMOST CHANGED AMERICA

BIBLIOGRAPHY

Rodolfo Acuna, *Occupied America: A History of Chicanos*. New York:
Harper & Row, 1981.

George Breitman, ed., *Malcolm X Speaks*. New York: Merit, 1969.

Robert Brisbane, *Black Activism*. Valley Forge, Pa: Judson Press, 1974.

Claybourne Carson, *Malcolm X: The FBI File*. New York:
Carroll & Graf, 1991.

Claybourne Carson, et al. *The Eyes on the Prize Civil Rights Reader*.
New York: Penguin, 1991.

E. U. Essien-Udom, *Black Nationalism*. Chicago: University of
Chicago Press, 1962.

Karl Evanzz, *The Judas Factor: The Plot to Kill Malcolm X*.
New York: Thunder's Mouth Press, 1992.

Michael Friedly, *Malcolm X; The Assassination*. New York:
Carroll & Graf, 1992.

David Garrow, *Bearing the Cross: Martin Luther King, Jr., and the
Southern Christian Leadership Conference*. New York:
Vintage, 1988.

Alex Haley, *The Autobiography of Malcolm X*. New York:
Grove, 1965.

Robert A. Hill, *Marcus Garvey: Life and Lessons*. Los Angeles:
University of California Press, 1987.

C.L.R. James, *The Black Jacobins*. New York: Vintage, 1963.

C. Eric Lincoln, *The Black Muslims in America*. Boston:
Beacon, 1961.

Louis Lomax, *When the Word Is Given*. Cleveland: World, 1963.

Tony Martin, *Race First*. Westport, Conn.: Greenwood, 1976.

Gordon Parks, "The White Devil's Day is Almost Over."
    Life, May 31, 1963.

Lynn Speakman, "Who Killed Malcolm X?" *The Valley Advocate*,
    Nov. 26, 1992, pp. 3–6.

William Tuttle, *Race Riot: Chicago, The Red Summer of 1919*.
    New York: Atheneum, 1970.

Theodore Vincent, *Black Power and the Garvey Movement*.
    San Francisco: Ramparts, 1972.

Theodore Vincent, "The Garveyite Parents of Malcolm X."
    The Black Scholar, Vol. 20, #2, April 1989.

C. Vann Woodward, *Origins of the New South*. Baton Rouge: Louisiana
    State University Press, 1967.

PHOTO CREDITS

THE HISTORY THAT MADE MALCOLM
(1925–1940)

Page 5: Gordon Parks; page 16: Station Hill Press; page 15: Abdul Aziz Omar; pages 16-17: Leavenworth Photographics, Inc.; page 17: Schomburg Center for Research in Black Culture, New York Public Library; page 18: Leavenworth Photographics, Inc.; page 18: Leavenworth Photographics, Inc.; page 18: Leavenworth Photographics, Inc.; page 19: Station Hill Press; page 20: James Van Der Zee; page 22: Abdul Aziz Omar; page 23: James Van Der Zee; page 24: Michigan Department of Health; page 24: UPI/Bettmann; page 27: Station Hill Press; page 28: Schomburg Center for Research in Black Culture, New York Public Library; page 29: James Van Der Zee; page 30: Abdul Aziz Omar; page 31: AP/Wide World; page 31: UPI/Bettmann; page 33: Kalamazoo Regional Psychiatric Hospital; page 32: Ingham County, Probate Court; page 34: Ingham County News, courtesy of Mason High School Library; page 34: Abdul Aziz Omar; page 35: Abdul Aziz Omar; page 35: Abdul Aziz Omar.

FROM CRIME TO CONSCIOUSNESS
(1941–1952)

Page 37: Commonwealth of Massachusetts/Dept. of Corrections; page 46: Abdul Aziz Omar; page 47: Courtesy of Ray Barron; page 47: Courtesy of Ray Barron; page 48: Magnum Photos; page 48: Schomburg Center for Research in Black Culture, New York Public Library; page 49: Schomburg Center for Research in Black Culture, New York Public Library; page 50: Schomburg Center for Research in Black Culture, New York Public Library; page 51: Muslim Mosque, O.A.A.U. Inc.—Malcolm X, Collins/Little Family Archives; page 51: Malcolm Jarvis; page 52: Security Pacific National Bank Photograph Collection/Los Angeles Public Library; page 53: National Archives; page 53: George Strock, Life Magazine, © Time Warner, Inc.; page 53: UPI/Bettmann; page 53: UPI/Bettmann; page 54: UPI/Bettmann; page 54: UPI/Bettmann; page 55: Station Hill Press; page 56: Courtesy of Detroit Police Dept.; page 56: Schomburg Center for Research in Black Culture, New York Public Library (Morgan & Marvin Smith Portfolio); page 56: Schomburg Center for Research in Black Culture, New York Public Library, (Gordon Anderson Collection); page 56: Frank Driggs Collection/Magnum Photos; page 57: Boston Globe Map, courtesy of

D. Butler; page 58: Commonwealth of Massachusetts/Superior Court Records; page 58: Commonwealth of Massachusetts/Superior Court Records; page 59: Boston Public Library/Print Dept.; page 59: Commonwealth of Massachusetts/Dept. of Corrections; page 60: Schomburg Center for Research in Black Culture, New York Public Library; page 60: UPI/Bettmann; page 61: Schomburg Center for Research in Black Culture, New York Public Library, (Afro-American Newspapers Archives and Research Center/Thurgood Marshall Library, Bowie State University); page 62: Commonwealth of Massachusetts/Dept. of Corrections; page 62: Courtesy of *The Muslim Journal*; page 63: Boston Public Library/Print Dept.; page 64: Commonwealth of Massachusetts/Dept. of Corrections; page 65: Society for the Preservation of New England Antiquities; page 66: Schomburg Center for Research in Black Culture, New York Public Library; page 67: Schomburg Center for Research in Black Culture, New York Public Library.

GROWING AND OUTGROWING THE NATION
(1953–1963)

Page 69: Eve Arnold/Magnum Photos; page 96: Black Images; page 97: Eve Arnold/Magnum Photos; page 98: Schomburg Center for Research in Black Culture, New York Public Library; page 99: Schomburg Center for Research in Black Culture, New York Public Library; page 99: Schomburg Center for Research in Black Culture, New York Public Library; page 101: UPI/Bettmann; page 100: Eve Arnold/Magnum Photos; page 102: UPI/Bettmann; page 102: Gordon Parks; page 103: Eve Arnold/Magnum Photos; page 105: Schomburg Center for Research in Black Culture, New York Public Library; page 106: Archive Photos/Richard Saunders; page 106: Eve Arnold/Magnum Photos; page 107: Eve Arnold/Magnum Photos; page 107: Courtesy of *The Muslim Journal*; page 108: Carl Nesfield/Pathfinder Press; page 108: Schomburg Center for Research in Black Culture, New York Public Library; page 109: UPI/Bettmann; page 110: Courtesy of *The Muslim Journal*; page 110: Archive Phots; page 111: Gordon Parks; page 112: Ted Russell/Life Magazine © Time Warner Inc.; page 113: Ted Russell/Life Magazine © Time Warner Inc.; page 113: Robert L. Haggins; page 114: Robert Parent/Pathfinder Press; page 114: UPI/Bettmann; page 114: Robert L. Haggins; page 116: Archive Photos; page 116: Archive Photos; page 117: Gordon Parks; page 118: Archive Photos/Richard Saunders; page 118: Gordon Parks; page 119: Archive Photos/Richard Saunders;

page 120: Archive Photos/Richard Saunders; page 121: Eve Arnold/Magnum Photos; page 122: Gordon Parks; page 123: Robert L. Haggins; page 122: Gordon Parks; page 124: Schomburg Center for Research in Black Culture, New York Public Library, (Richard Saunders); page 125: Robert L. Haggins; page 126: Courtesy of *The Muslim Journal*; page 127: Courtesy of *The Muslim Journal*; page 128: Courtesy of *The Muslim Journal*; page 129: UPI/Bettmann; page 130: Eve Arnold/Magnum Photos; page 131: Eve Arnold/Magnum Photos; page 133: AP/Wide World; page 132: Courtesy of *The Muslim Journal*; page 135: Archive Photos; page 135: Eve Arnold/Magnum Photos; page 135: Eve Arnold/Magnum Photos; page 136: Courtesy of the F.B.I.; page 137: AP/Wide World; page 138: UPI/Bettmann; page 139: Robert Parent/Pathfinder Press; page 141: Robert L. Haggins; page 140: UPI/Bettmann; page 140: UPI/Bettmann; page 142: UPI/Bettmann; page 142: Charles Moore/Black Star; page 144: Schomburg Center for Research in Black Culture, New York Public Library, (courtesy of Milton Meltzer); page 145: *Muhammad Speaks*, courtesy of *The Muslim Journal*; page 146: UPI/Bettmann; page 146: UPI/Bettmann.

FIGHTING ON THREE FRONTS
(1964–1965)

Page 149: John Launois/Black Star; page 166: Robert L. Haggins; page 167: *Muhammad Speaks,* courtesy of *The Muslim Journal*; page 167: Schomburg Center for Research in Black Culture, New York Public Library, (Laurence Henry Collection); page 169: Schomburg Center for Research in Black Culture, New York Public Library; page 169: Robert L. Haggins; page 170: Robert Parent/Pathfinder Press; page 171: UPI/Bettmann; page 172: Eli Finer/Pathfinder Press; page 173: UPI/Bettmann; page 174: Courtesy of *The Muslim Journal*; page 175: *Playboy* Magazine, © 1963/Richard Saunders; page 176: Archive Photos; page 177: John Launois/Black Star; page 178: Alice Windom; page 179: Alice Windom; page 180: Alice Windom; page 181: Alice Windom; page 181: John Launois/Black Star; page 182: Archive Photos; page 183: Robert Parent/Pathfinder Press; page 184: John Launois/Black Star; page 185: *New York Post*; page 186: Ed Druck/Impact Visuals; page 187: UPI/Bettmann; page 191: *Playboy* Magazine © 1963/Richard Saunders; page 188: John Launois/Black Star; page 000: UPI/Bettmann; page 189: AP/Wide World; page 190: Schomburg Center for Research in Black Culture, New York Public Library; page 190: Doug Harris; page 193: UPI/Bettmann; page 193: Archive Photos; page 192: John Launois/Black Star; page 194: Schomburg Center for Research in Black Culture, New

York Public Library; page 195: Robert Parent/Pathfinder Press; page 196: Robert L. Haggins; page 197: *Muhammad Speaks*, courtesy of *The Muslim Journal*; page 198: UPI/Bettmann; page 199: John Launois/Black Star; page 200: P.H. Polk, Tuskegee University Archives, courtesy of Pathfinder Press; page 200: AP/Wide World; page 201: Schomburg Center for Research in Black Culture, New York Public Library, (Laurence Henry Collection); page 202: UPI/Bettmann; page 202: Robert L. Haggins; page 203: Greg Harris, *Life* Magazine © Time Warner Inc.; page 204: John Launois/Black Star; page 205: UPI/Bettmann; page 206: UPI/Bettmann; page 206: UPI/Bettmann; page 207: UPI/Bettman; page 208: AP/Wide World; page 208: UPI/Bettmann; page 209: UPI/Bettmann; page 210: Archive Photos; page 210: UPI/Bettmann; page 211: UPI/Bettmann; page 212: UPI/Bettmann; page 212: AP/Wide World; page 213: Schomburg Center for Research in Black Culture, New York Public Library, (Laurence Henry Collection); page 214: Robert Parent/Pathfinder Press; page 214: UPI/Bettmann; page 215: Adger Cowans/Black Images; page 216: UPI/Bettmann; page 216: Matt Heron/Black Star; page 217: UPI/Bettmann.

EPILOGUE:
THE MAN WHO ALMOST CHANGED AMERICA

Page 219: Russel Shorto/Agincourt Press; page 225: EMI Records; page 225: Douglass Rowell for the Zomba Recording Group; page 226: Klytus Smith/Black Images; page 227: Ted Soqui/Impact Visuals; page 229: Andrew Lichtenstein/Impact Visual; page 228: Hiroji Kubota/Magnum Photos; page 229: Linda Rosier/Impact Visuals; page 230: Clark Jones/Impact Visuals; page 231: David Vita/Impact Visuals; page 232: Kirk Condyles/Impact Visuals; page 233: Forty Acres And A Mule Productions; page 234: John Bounting/Impact Visuals; page 235: Walter Bartolomei.

MALCOLM X: MAKE IT PLAIN
Production Staff

Henry E. Hampton — Executive Producer

Orlando Bagwell — Producer/Director/Co-Writer

Judy Richardson — Co-Producer

Steve Fayer — Co-Writer

Meredith Woods — Line Producer

Denise Greene — Associate Producer

Jean Tsien — Editor

Sandra Christie — Associate Editor

Karen M. McMullen — Assistant Editor

Robin Espinola, Rachel Harding, Greg Hunter, Daisy E. Jackson, Andre Namphy — Researchers

Barnard Jaffier — Apprentice Editor

Ralph Dustin — Production Assistant